I0445278

THE 7 EASY STEPS TO ANGER MANAGEMENT FOR PARENTS WITH TODDLERS

HOW TO STOP STRESSING SO MUCH AND START ENJOYING PARENTHOOD

RAFFAEL LYON & S.K. BRAGA

CONTENTS

INTRODUCTION

By Raffael & S.K Braga

WHAT A PARENT IS...

Being a parent is being there

Through the tantrums,

The milestones and the tears,

Being a parent means that you love that little person who you created,

More than you could ever love yourself or anybody else!

You'd readily lose sleep to comfort them from their nightmares,

You would risk your own life for that tiny person,

You'd surely die to save them if you needed to.

Being a parent is never a burden, it's loving somebody else,

Wholeheartedly and unconditionally,

For eternity!

Being a parent to your child is not a job, it's a privilege,

Cherish it!

— UNKNOWN

This wasn't the kind of family you anticipated; it's far from the home of your dreams.

You wanted a peaceful household, a family where you were your kids' best friend.

It was a family where your children wouldn't feel the world crashing down when they mistakenly took a wrong turn.

A family that would be a haven for you, your spouse, and your children – all of you standing back-to-back and conquering the world together.

Perhaps you recently took a trip to the past and saw an image of your younger self. You saw what you wanted as a kid. You felt, once again, the emotions and the cravings for an empathetic parent. A parent who could step into your shoes and realize you were just a little kid trying to make sense of the world and how it works. A parent who would not flare up at simple mistakes because, really - kids should be permitted to be kids, right?

So, you vowed to be different; you would start a different trend. You determined your family would be a loving and happy one.

But this hasn't been the case lately.

More often than not, you've found yourself behaving in ways you don't want to. As though you were in a pool of quicksand- trying to get out of this terrible parenting style. Still, the harder you try, the more you watch yourself sink.

Not to say that this is your fault. If anything, it's far from that. You don't want to be an angry parent. No. You don't. The desire to run a home built on trust and empathy rather than fear and anxiety is still as strong as when you were a kid. If anyone could take a peep into your heart, what would be seen is the yearning to have a special parent-child bond with your little one.

And then, there's your job too. You want to spend loads of time with your children, but your hours consume you to keep the bills from engulfing the family.

Could there possibly be a way out of this mess?

What if we told you we've found one?

Suppose there is anyone who could understand you, probably us. Having been married for over eight years, we've figured out how to raise kids very composedly while still enjoying our personal lives. As a family, we've explored the world together. In a way, we've learned how to balance work time and family time. Better still, we've learned to keep our temper in check when communicating with our children.

Although we look like the perfect family, what you don't see is that we weren't always like this.

About three years ago, we noticed how we were easily inclined to yell at our toddler. A day didn't pass by without one of us losing our cool. Parenting was more of hell than heaven. Even though we didn't want this, we couldn't help ourselves. It felt as though we were configured to act that way; we were configured to naturally respond with so much anger.

This trend continued for a while. Months upon months, we found ourselves falling into the same pits. We wanted a calm family but what we did took us down the opposite path. Needless to say, we were not enjoying parenthood much. We thought this would be the case our entire lives. We thought we would never have a happy family. We thought we would raise our kids how our parents brought us up (which wasn't pleasant).

Fortunately, something life-changing happened to us.

We came across a set of strategies that raised our hope. Instantly, we began implementing these strategies- one day at a time. Then, after a couple of months, there it was: the family we had always hoped for, taking shape right before our eyes!

We've concluded that it wasn't only these strategies that helped us form an empathic family. The personal parenting lessons we picked along the way also played a vital role. Although we've been together for eight years, we've been parents for only five years. As a result, we've come to terms with practical parenting lessons and tips you won't find in just any book or website during this timeframe.

About four months ago, Kelly, a family friend, said something that shocked us. It was over dinner when she revealed how angry she was at herself. We had our first kid about the same period Kelly was also having hers. However, she believed our families were significantly apart. She commented on how free and calm we were with our kids and acted like our kids' playmates. Although she tried replicating the same with her children, she couldn't bring herself to relate with them as we did with ours.

So, we introduced the exact set of strategies you are about to read to Kelly. Two months ago, she sent us a text telling us how helpful the anger management tips were to her and her husband.

Like Kelly, we believe many parents are out there looking for a way out of their misery (especially if your kids are in the terrible twos). That's why we decided to pen these secrets down on paper.

In the past, you may have searched on the internet about being a better parent. How do you manage your temper when dealing with your kids? How do you avoid being like your parents? Since you are reading this book, our wild guess is that you've not found your answer- or maybe, you've not found a practical one focused on toddlers yet. Luckily, here we plan to answer the questions you are asking. Much better, we plan to do so in a very realistic way.

In this book, you will find a detailed 7-step approach toward curbing your anger and forging a relationship that other parents could only dream of with your child. This isn't a random compilation of tips on being a better parent. Instead, this is our journey put down in words. What you have in your hands is five years' worth of parenting lessons condensed into a book. Here, we will be giving you a peek into our parenting lives and the lessons we've picked up along the way.

We will be looking at anger from different angles- from your view as a parent to the toddler's perspective and then from the environmental standpoint.

A shortcut. A mentorship. An accessible route—call it whatever you wish—but surely, after reading this book, you won't be making the same mistakes we made. Most people don't know that dealing with anger is not just about what they are doing- it could also be about what they are not doing.

For instance, are you aware that managing anger doesn't begin with teaching your toddler how to stop triggering you? Of course, a step talks about helping toddlers deal with the developmental phase they are stuck in. Even still, dealing with anger begins with you. This book will show you how simple lifestyle changes can significantly improve your anger management ordeal.

We will reveal the step-by-step approach to a manner of parenting that transformed us from being parents who were stuck in a never-ending cycle of rage and guilt to being thoughtful and loving parents.

Envision the home of your dreams: a family fueled by love and compassion. A home where kids are brought up without the fear of an angry parent. Parents that know how to reach down to their kids without yelling. Decide in your heart that you will put to practice everything you learn here, and your dream home will become a reality. However, remember that it is not just about reading- it is about doing.

The advantages of this book span beyond helping you manage your temper. As you already know, the happenings in the early years of a child's life will play a huge role in determining that child's attitude towards life. As a result of these tips, you will also be able to raise confident kids. Kids who are free to air their opinions about issues surrounding them. These kids won't fear what people say or think about them; as kids, they weren't shamed when they made mistakes and won't be scared to say the right things now that they are adults.

In Mathew Jacobsen's words, "behind every young child who believes in themselves is a parent who believed in them first." So, determine to shape your kids into the adults you want to see tomorrow. This book will provide positive parenting tips to help you forge excellent connections with your little ones. Knowing these secrets, alongside a relentless determination to be a better parent, will produce jaw-dropping results that will leave you in awe of what you've become.

See this book as an opportunity to change the terrible trend of lousy parenting in your family tree. Your parents made this error you see yourself completing. And probably, their parents also made these same mistakes. You shouldn't go down the same path now that it's your turn.

And because you are armed with this book, you won't.

A FREE GIFT FOR MY READERS!

Included with your purchase of this book is your free copy of
7 Morning Rituals That Help Parents Thrive Daily

Scan the QR code below to receive your free copy:

1

IT STARTS WITH YOU

I t feels like you've changed, right?

You could swear that the "you" who existed just before your child was born differs from the "you" reading this book right now.

Because that seems like the only logical answer to how you went from being a caring, ready-to-face-the-world expecting parent to a yelling wrecking ball. Even though it might not have been a conscious decision, your dream was to raise the perfect Instagram family- a family at least different from the one you grew up in.

During childbirth, you could still feel this rising within your mind- ever stronger, ever resilient.

However, things began falling apart once your child hit one, hell broke loose, and you couldn't contain it. It felt as though someone used a vacuum to extract all the grit you've got in your body, wrapped it together, and flushed it down the drain.

Now, you watch yourself repeating – time and again- the same things your parents did. You see yourself yelling at your child without premeditation- you just do it.

And that's what you hate the most.

Why can't you stop yourself from doing what you don't want to do? Why does it seem like you don't have control over your emotions?

Somewhere lurking in your mind is a belief that the reason you display so much anger is the developmental phase your child is presently in. In a way, you are correct. However, that's not the whole picture.

You don't know that this ordeal began long ago- long before you realized anything was happening. You still do some things that bite you in the back, causing you to yell at your child. This, and many more, are what we will reveal in this chapter.

Once you understand the components of anger, you will be equipped with the right mindset to apply the practical steps that have been enlisted in this book.

Let us prove to you that, indeed, the path to recovery begins with you.

UNPREPARED ANGER

Ask any parent, and they would testify that having children changes your life forever. There's a giant hole in your heart that you did not know existed until your child came along. Then, suddenly, you feel a connection with another human- a connection you've never experienced.

Every parent can relate to this, especially mothers.

Recent scientific study has proven that this connection could be more literal. When a woman is pregnant, there is some sort of exchange of cells between the mother and the child through the placenta (which connects the mother to the child). For both parties, these cells distribute themselves throughout the body, incorporating themselves into the organs of the mother and child. Known as fetal microchimerism, this phenomenon alters the genetic makeup of mothers.

This might be why a bond, which you cannot explain, exists between you and your child. Maybe this is why you feel so emotionally attached to your child.

Many noticeable changes occurred from the moment you got the news that a baby's on the way- from the relentless mood swings to the "glorious" morning sickness, from a growing belly to constant fatigue. However, some silent changes also appear in the woman's body. One of which, as we've mentioned, is fetal microchimerism. Another is the shrinking of the woman's brain.

Yes, your brain shrank while you were pregnant. The effects of this shrinkage can still be observed two years after you give birth.

While this might sound like something detrimental, it might have been one of the changes you should be grateful for.

While you were pregnant, there was a massive production of sex steroids: progesterone and estrogen. The only other period, in a human's life, like this experience is puberty. During puberty, these hormones would cause enormous changes in the brain of teenagers, one of which is the pruning of cells. Cells that are not needed are pruned, causing the brain to become more functional.

As a result of these sex steroids, something similar occurs during pregnancy.

The part of your brain targeted is that which has the strongest response when you look at your child. In other words, this part of your brain is pruned to become much more active. Little wonder you feel so emotionally connected to the tiny human tornado that consistently makes the home a mess! Finally, you understand the phrase "love is blind" because you see yourself loving (to the extreme) someone who finds so much joy in driving you crazy.

If the thought that your brain shrank will keep you up at night, take it this way: your brain found a way to become more efficient and intelligent. Think of it as a form of trimming the garden- it makes your home a little more organized. Because your brain neurons become more closely associated, it is easier for you to deal with a mother's emotional and mental require-ments. So, if it ever crossed your mind to bet that your brain isn't functioning how it used to "pre-baby," then do it- science got your back!

While these changes occur before the child is born, I'm sure you can testify of the changes when your child came into the world. Aside from shifting your goals and priorities, everyday tasks and obligations also took a U-turn.

For instance, your child's preferences automatically become yours. If you were a night person, you might see yourself turning into an early bird. Your routine becomes different because you need to incorporate your child's needs into your day. Everything becomes two times longer than it usually would be. You rarely have time for yourself- taking "me" time shifts from being spontaneous to being extremely intentional. Your standards for what a clean home should be swings from having a sparkling floor to a floor just free from the clutter of toys.

These would have a toll on your stress levels and emotional health. And sincerely, since you are human, a rise in your anger levels is quite...normal.

WHAT CAUSES ANGER?

Let's begin from the basics- Anger 101.

Like every other emotion, anger shouldn't be considered harmful. However, when put it side by side with other emotions such as happiness and hope, it settles for a negative reputation. Perhaps, because the outcomes of an angry human are primarily destructive rather than constructive, people have grown to associate anger with violence and aggression.

Just picture it. If you were to describe the scene of an angry individual, what words would you use?

"He was 'mad' another guy stepped on his toes."

"Her 'rage' was so obvious when her husband made a joke about marriage."

While society has made us believe anger is an emotion that should be eradicated from humanity, maybe we should look the other way. Perhaps we should consider why getting angry is not just good but very important in attaining our goals.

To start with, what's the origin of this emotion?

As people evolved, our emotions also evolved. The goal was survival, and specific "threats" hindered that. To keep us safe, we had to come up with an almost instant response when we sensed threats in our environments. This response is what we know today as anger.

While the goal might have evolved from survival to other advanced reasons such as having our wishes respected, not being talked down on, and generally maintaining our feeling of "importance," the threats to all of this are still very much all around us.

For instance, when your child refuses to stop throwing tantrums whenever you don't get a new toy at the store or when the little one resists your bedtime rules unless you spend half the night walking them to bed over and over, you have your wishes violated. As the parent, you should be the one setting the rules, right?

So, your child's actions threaten one of your core desires- feeling respected.

Consequently, you get frustrated. Why can't your child obey a simple instruction?

Then gradually, the frustration builds in you...and suddenly, you hit a breaking point. Before you realize what's going on, this primitive emotion- anger- decides it is about time to run the day and manifests itself as you throw yells at your 2-year-old.

Asides from this, there are other reasons why you get angry, some of which we will outline later. But first, we need you to understand this: anger itself is not destructive; it is how you express it that makes it wrong.

You should see anger as an emotion the body uses to feed our minds with information about how we **feel** in the moment. Anger is not inherently an aggressive emotion- in this case, anger is simply your body's way of telling you that you aren't in control of your child's behavior at that exact moment.

Again, anger manifests another of your core desires- control. It kicks in whenever you feel out of control by your child's actions. Rather than feeling helpless, anger helps you fulfill one of your innate needs- the desire to be in control. Therefore, you yell whenever you feel angry; it brings back that feeling of being behind the wheel in the New York City rush hour traffic.

However, there's this thing called emotional intelligence that kicks in when you learn how to process why you feel angry in that situation, and how to better express the raging anger you feel in your bones.

That said, aside from the tantrums your toddler throws, there are many other reasons you feel angry.

WHAT CAUSES YOU TO BE ANGRY?

Apart from exhaustion, there's something a bit more clinical such as primary emotions and secondary emotions battling in your mind. Primary emotions are our initial feeling to a situation, while secondary emotions are the reactions we have after our primary emotion.

For example, let's say you just got home from work and your child starts acting up. Your first emotion might be frustration and the reaction to it is you yell at your child. However, after you've had a chance to calm down and think about the situation, you might feel disappointed.

As a parent, you are saddled with so many responsibilities- keeping up with the bills, performing effectively at work, maintaining your relationships with close friends, raising your child in the best possible way...and a thousand more obligations while still ensuring your health doesn't take the hit. As a new parent, that's a lot on your plate. It is easy to get frustrated when you don't meet a certain standard you've set for yourself. Not just that- frustration can also set in due to your child's actions and inactions. And, if you have a partner, it might be hard to deal with when you don't agree on everything, especially about how to raise your child.

These frustrations can easily translate into outbursts. In this case, frustrations would be the primary emotion, while the outbursts would be the secondary emotion. And indeed, it is easier to express outbursts than to express frustration. Expressing frustration might make you vulnerable because it involves you coming open about your feelings to the individuals involved. However, the outburst gives you an instant sense of control (remember what we said about our human craving for control?). Hence, masking your deeper feeling of frustration with outbursts seems like the easier path to take.

Action tip

Take some time to reflect on your past outbursts. Was your anger a genuine primary emotion, or was it because you were frustrated? Or were there any primary emotions aside from frustration that could have fueled your anger?

Since angry outbursts are easier to express, it can prevent you from dealing with the root cause of your emotions. So, in attempting to tackle your anger, you must be intentional about knowing how you feel; you need to work on becoming self-aware. A good way of doing this is by taking mindfulness exercises.

Mindfulness involves being present in the moment rather than being caught up in your thoughts. Although this could help you recognize how you feel in the moment, being mindful is not as easy as it sounds.

Recent studies show that we have more than 6,000 thoughts every day. That's roughly 6.5 thoughts a minute and one thought every 10 seconds. Honestly, that's a lot. Most times, we don't even realize we are having thoughts.

For instance, you are presently having a thought as you read this.

And now, you just realized you had a thought- oops, there goes another one.

On and on and on... you are more lost in your head than you think.

Hence, staying in the present moment and staying in touch with the things that are going on around you (sights and sounds) and the things going on inside you (thoughts and feelings) requires that you put in some measure of effort. Mindfulness requires intentionality but it doesn't have to be difficult.

A great way of developing your mindfulness muscle is by taking mindfulness exercises.

Mindfulness exercise

- *Set a timer for 10-20 minutes.*
- *Find a comfortable place to sit or lay. If you choose to sit, ensure you sit up with your back straight and shoulders down.*
- *Close your eyes and bring your attention to your breathing. Is your breathing shallow or deep?*
- *Take a deep breath. Focus your mind on how it feels to have air rushing through your nostrils.*
- *Now, take your attention to your belly. Notice how it rises and falls with each breath you take. Continue to take deep breaths and immerse yourself entirely in the experience.*
- *Remain in that position until your timer goes off.*

You will notice how your mind wanders off as you take this exercise. It is entirely normal for this to happen. That's the purpose of this exercise- to see it happen. You would catch yourself having thoughts without realizing when the thoughts began. Whenever this happens, nip the thoughts right in their bud and bring yourself back to being aware of your breath- the present moment.

Take time out to practice this every day, preferably at the beginning of your day. As you consistently engage in this exercise, you will see yourself taking an observer approach to your thoughts and feelings during the day. It will become easier to know exactly how you feel right at the moment.

The first step to solving a problem is becoming aware there is a problem. Likewise, the first step to anger management is learning how to process your emotions. Only by addressing your emotions can we hope to resolve future situations in a better way.

A crucial part of doing so is being non-judgmental about how you feel. If you feel frustrated by how many tantrums your toddler throws, that's fine. If you feel frustrated because your partner doesn't seem to under-stand your point of view, that's normal. The reason you feel this way is because you are human. And, it is okay to feel how you feel!

Next, you want to communicate your emotions. You could do this by talking to the individual involved or a neutral person. Better still, express yourself in writing by having a mood journal. Keep your journal with you every time you feel a "negative" emotion, dig deep into why you feel it, and put it down on paper. This way, you can reflect on the cause of your primary emotions and identify triggers of these emotions and begin to address them. Doing this will help mitigate your anger sooner than you think!

BODILY HEALTH CAUSES OF ANGER

▷ **Lack of sleep**

Without the need for any scientific studies, we can all agree that we do everything less efficiently when we don't sleep well. But science does back it up. The fact is its undeniable how much sleep deprivation affects our parenting.

Still, tackling this constant exhaustion isn't relatively easy. To many parents, being exhausted comes with the parenthood package- newborns will wake up to eat, and toddlers will wake up due to separation anxiety. So, how is it possible to even begin to tackle this?

First, add sleep time to your daily plans. Like anything that is important to you, prioritize it and do not leave when you doze off up to chance. When making your schedule for the day, factor in "sleep-time." If you have the ability, a great way to catch up on sleep is going to bed when your toddler is having their afternoon nap.

Action tip

If you are working full-time, could you eat from your desk a little earlier while working and take a nap in your office or somewhere safe during lunchtime?

Additionally, you don't want to go too hard on yourself when tired. Of course, productivity would mean that you try to reply to emails while cooking dinner. However, on days when you find yourself feeling burnt out, pause being productive and just live. When you consciously choose to let go of all the little details and focus on one thing, it makes it easier to respond calmly in the event your toddler does something that could trigger your anger.

Lastly, when you are tired, stop being a parent. Yeah, that sounds a little absurd because, really, that's who you are by default. However, after a long, sleepless night, when you wake up in the morning, decide that today won't be a day of proactive parenthood. This means you won't be focused on giving your toddler any lessons on why this and that is not a good way of getting things done. If you try being a proactive parent when you are tired, you may respond more aggressively than you think. So, chill out and give yourself some slack.

▷ Mental health

Anger could present a symptom of certain mental health conditions such as depression or OCD. While depression refers to a constant feeling of sadness lasting at least two weeks or more, OCD, which stands for obsessive-compulsive disorder, describes the urges to do something repeatedly and compulsively. What's common, however, is how anger could be a manifesting symptom of both depression and OCD.

Asides from these, other mental health conditions could be an underlying cause of anger. This would include conditions such as grief and bipolar disorder. Before ruling out the possibility that a mental health condition could be the cause raging anger, you should visit a professional if you think the state of your mind might be affecting your moods.

▷ Physical health

You've probably heard this a thousand times, but don't mind us reiterating it: Exercise and diet play a vital role in alleviating almost all negatives in our lives. From helping us prevent obesity to keeping our backs free from pain, new research suggests that exercise releases endorphins helping us deal with our moods, especially our angry moods. Not just that. You don't need a study to make you believe how much a good meal could help alleviate the anger that comes with hunger pangs.

Hence, make it a duty to care for your physical health. Slot in some exercises into your morning or afternoon routine and ensure you choose proper nutritious meals daily. Over time, this will help you manage the anger you feel and allow you react more calmly.

SOCIAL CAUSES OF ANGER

▷ **Unrealistic expectations**

With the advent of the internet and social media, the bars we set for our personal and family life has taken an unrealistic jump. We often base our idea of what a family should be on what we see on social media. So, when our children or partners don't fit into the perfect picture, it frustrates us.

However, the reality isn't always filtered like in social media. And, to free yourself from unrealistic expectations, you must choose to break the chain of a "perfect social media family." Between us here- there is no such thing as a perfect family.

In your case, it might not be social media- it could be the family next door. They seem to live the perfect life- a son or daughter who doesn't throw as many tantrums as yours and a more caring partner. But you must realize that no two families are the same. Comparing yourself- or your family- with a seemingly perfect one would mean denying yourself of the uniqueness in you and setting yourself up for heartbreak when your child goes against the ideal image in your head.

Like other humans, your child will make mistakes. Your child will spoil the new clothes you just got. Your toddler won't finish dinner in time for you to do the dishes every day. Learning to see the humanity in your child will help you be calmer and patient when they display their imperfect side. Choose to see your family as a progressing one rather than a perfect one. If you do this, when the mistakes come- because they are sure to come- you will be able to deal with them gently, lovingly and with laughter.

Action tip

Reflect: What unrealistic expectations do you have for your children? Bear in mind that your child is only a child. Don't judge your child through the lens of an adult.

Another way of dealing with unrealistic expectations is through the simple act of gratitude. Here's how: Since we live in a society that promotes perfection over progress, we often find ourselves in a loop of self-agony where we focus on what's not right rather than what we have going right. We become people who default to being unhappy about what we don't have rather than grateful for what we do have.

And honestly, gratitude isn't just an action- it is a state of mind. Gratitude is a decision to remain happy for the things that went according to plan, rather than focusing on the minute details that don't go just how we planned.

So, how on earth does being grateful help you deal with anger?

Well, if your anger springs up from unrealistic expectations, gratitude gives you the ability to focus on all your positive traits while giving you the space to acknowledge the negative features you need to improve. In the end, it is an act of self-love and self-gracefulness. Towards others, gratitude helps you stop being so critical about their actions. It enables you to see the big picture of who the person is and how happy you are to have that individual in your life. In this case, the individual might be your child. Gratitude creates in you a well of joy that becomes easy to quench the raging fire of anger when it comes.

How do you develop gratitude?

A proven way of getting this habit flowing within your veins is by having a gratitude journal. As the name implies, a gratitude journal is where you jot down the things you are grateful for every day. If you have a problem, dig deep into finding a reason to be thankful that the problem exists. For instance, if your toddler can't just seem to keep clothes on when in public, choose to be grateful; you have such a smart child who knows how to take off their clothes.

Even though gratitude is a vital tool, you should know it is not a magic pill. You won't immediately stop being angry the moment you start being grateful. Eventually, as you practice it every day, the habit will slip into your veins, and you will find yourself being thankful for the very things you were once angry about. Before you know it, it will all come together!

▷ Cluttered lives

To be overly time conscious and get more items off our to-do list, we often sacrifice our peace at the expense of being a guru at time management. You answer the emails in the bathroom, create a perfect pitch while in the queue, and do all your freelance jobs while spending time with your child in the backyard.

Don't get us wrong- being efficient is fantastic. That's a trait you would want your child to pick up from you. However, trying to tick every single item off your list most likely will overwhelm you. And honestly, stress and anger fuel each other. In an instant, you could watch yourself explode at a little mistake your child makes because you failed to meet a self-imposed deadline. Here the stress of your deadline fueled your angry explosion.

Let's be true to ourselves- our toddlers will always do things that make us angry. Since they don't fully grasp how things work in the real world, they will act in ways that seem entirely illogical to us. And to respond calmly, we must be in an uncluttered state of mind. This can be possible only if we decide to focus on one thing at a time.

It involves saying no "as often" as you say yes. No to more activities but yes to fewer events on your calendar. Doing this will solve a crucial part of the puzzle- your to-do list. There isn't an award for the most productive parent in the world (unless there is one, we are not aware of). So how about letting go of trying to be *the one?* Spoiler alert, if there is such award, it would come with the most stressed-out parent award as well.

We know, we used to be that parent- The most productive stressed-out parents in the world. And it wasn't until we decided to careless of what everyone else thought and to make our life be as simple as possible that things began to turn around for us. Now, the main components that our daily to-do list is built on, consist of three things:

1. What is our 3-5 priorities today? We each write it down.
2. Less is more; more is less. Multitasking is a myth, don't worry, be happy.
3. Execute our priorities. Life will always throw curve balls at you, but if everything is a priority than nothing is a priority.

Everything else we choose to add is weighted against these three core daily goals.

Action tip

Reflect: What can you do less of daily, so you can enjoy more of parenthood?

PATTERNS OF ANGER MANAGEMENT

If you grew up in an environment that managed anger poorly, you may have picked up the same traits. Anger runs through generations. Assuming it doesn't stem from mental health issues, many mental health experts would agree that anger is a learned behavior. Hence, most people can trace their anger traits to someone in their family- their father, mother, sibling, or grandparent, who negatively expressed their anger.

Remember, we previously established that all emotions are expected, including anger. However, anger would be considered detrimental when expressed in unhealthy ways, such as yelling and shouting. Usually, the child's family teaches them what to do when they feel certain emotions. Likewise, how you react to anger might be an in-built method of approach.

While some learned to bottle it all up, others knew that a massive explosion of yells was the best way to express anger. Either way, the truth is that once you recognize what patterns of anger management exist in your family, you can choose to break the destructive cycle; you can decide not to pass it down to your children.

Action tip

Reflect: Does anger run in your family? Can you recognize a family member who exhibited the trait? State in your words how the individual reacted to rage? Did this individual bottle it all in until there was a giant explosion? Renew your decision not to take the same path the person took.

STRUCTURAL CAUSES OF ANGER

Structural anger is often the result of feeling over-whelmed or stressed. This can be caused by a number of factors, including financial problems, work stress, or simply having too much to do. When you are already feeling stretched thin, it doesn't take much for your toddler to push you over the edge. Whether it's throwing a tantrum in public or refusing to go to bed, toddlers can be trying at the best of times. But some-times, we may be stressed about something that has nothing to do with our child, yet still we end up taking it out on them.

No matter what the cause of your anger is, it's impor-tant to know that often losing your temper with your toddler can damage your relationship and cause them to feel scared of you. If you're finding it hard to stay calm, an easy way to help you keep your anger in check is to take a deep breaths and count to ten. You can also try walking away for a minute or two to give yourself time to cool down.

If after implementing this, you're still feeling angry, it's best to talk to someone about it, such as a friend or family member. Bottling up your anger will only make it worse in the long run. While parents will always get angry at times, it's important to try and keep it under control for the sake of your child.

As you know by now, stopping the trend of anger requires more than a passing wish. So, take some time to undergo some introspection. Come to terms with why you act the way you do. Then, work on implementing solutions a step at a time. It requires a determination to keep trying your best to get our heads out of the waters anytime we make mistakes. And to help you not to give up, let's look at the effects of anger on your children.

EFFECTS OF ANGER ON YOUR CHILDREN

You are your child's hero. From birth, your child becomes entirely dependent on you for a sense of self and a model to look up to. It goes without saying-anger itself isn't a destructive emotion. Everyone feels angry at some point. However, as a parent, you must take extra caution in manifesting your anger.

If done wrongly, your child could potentially develop defenses against you. Your child could become accustomed to your yells and the corrections you intend to give won't have a lasting impact on them.

Again, as we've previously established, anger runs through generations since it is a learned trait. You don't want your children growing up to become angry adults. If you grew up in an environment filled with angry people, you know how it affected you later. If you learned your anger from someone you looked up to, it is time to break the trend. And doing so comes with a lot of benefits.

First, you unconsciously teach your children how to deal with anger correctly. As a model to your growing kid, your kid will emulate you and your behaviors. Coping with anger the right way can be compared to giving your child a template for going through life. Your child will come across many situations that will test their temper. And if the right path is learned from you, life becomes much more manageable.

Secondly, you promote a better relationship with your child. Regardless of whether your intentions for yelling were good or bad, your child will see you as an angry parent. And ask any child- no one wants to be vulnerable with an angry parent. Every child craves a parent who knows how to guide them respectfully and heal them without causing more pain. If your child cannot trust you will speak calmly, your child will respond with avoidance and withdrawal. Once you deal with your anger issues, in the long run, your child will begin to see you as a haven- a person with whom they can be completely open and feel no shame. I bet you want to be that kind of mom or dad!

See this section as a sort of motivational section. When you feel down or discouraged about whether you can break the family trend or not, read through this section again. Your child needs you to step up to the challenge. You can do this. If we could, you can too!

IDENTIFYING AND BREAKING THE CYCLE OF ANGER

Up till now, we've discussed the emotional components of anger. However, there's also a physical response to anger- and it exists in five stages. Understanding the stages of this biological response might be a key to breaking the progression and gaining back control of your emotion.

The first stage is the **trigger stage**. Here, you receive a trigger- in this case, from your child. Your toddler hits a friend when playing or scatters the toys all around the home to defy you. Your brain receives this trigger, your physiological system senses this as a threat, and your body begins to prepare for action.

Then, there is the **escalation stage**. Here, the physical response to the threat sensed is heightened. Blood is diverted from your gut to your muscles, and they become tense, your eyes become enlarged, the pitch of your voice is altered, and at times, your stance changes- all signs of your physiological system preparing for action.

Next, there is the **crisis stage.** At this point, your decisions cannot be trusted as the quality of your judgment is hampered. All you are concerned about is survival- which in this case, might mean having your child do this your way!

The fourth stage is called the **recovery stage, which** then kicks in. Gradually, the quality of your judgment returns, and you gain consciousness of what you just did. The adrenaline rush escapes your bloodstream and leaves you to deal with the harsh reality of a child crying from your yells.

Lastly, you enter the **post-crisis depression stage.** Here, your heart rate might be deep below normal and other emotions secondary to your anger take over. You feel guilty for yelling at your child and regret how you handled the situation.

When you are angry, your goal is to assess what phase of anger you are in immediately. Then, do something to counter that stage. For instance, aim to calm down if you are at the escalation stage. Since your judgment would be undergoing a downward spiral, you don't want to say things or make quick decisions. Count to 10 quietly in your head, and don't utter a word.

If your child behaves in ways you don't understand, your child's behavior might act as a trigger. Self-reflect on the behaviors you believe triggered your anger and use the action plan below when faced with a similar situation. In the next chapter, you will learn why children act the way they do. After reading the next chapter, your child's behavior won't be much of a mystery.

But first, check out these actionable steps to managing your anger in the heat of the moment.

YOUR GO-TO ACTION PLAN

Let's be honest with each other: you don't care how you became an angry parent in the spur of the moment. What you desperately want is to stop being angry. Simple.

So, here's how you can start:

- Count to 10 in your head and imagine a relaxing place. If possible, go online and search for inspirational art or pictures of relaxing areas. Stare at the art or picture so many times that the image becomes ingrained into you. Whenever you feel anger rising, recall the art or photo you chose. This could save you from the guilt and regret that trails your yells, as silly as this may sound.

- Sit down and take seven to ten deep breaths. Remember we discussed a mindfulness exercise? This is where it comes in handy. Science proves that taking deep breaths is a great way to counter your physiological response to your triggers.

- Once you are calm, ask yourself what caused the emotions. Dig deep until you find out the primary emotion behind your anger. You can deal with the primary emotion (perhaps, frustration) more healthily when you find it.

INTERACTIVE ELEMENT- SUMMARY

We've covered the causes of anger and the patterns of anger management.

However, for a long-term approach to curbing anger, you might want to see a therapist if you learned anger as a child or believe your anger might be a symptom of an underlying mental illness.

Secondly, as we have discussed, you need to work towards reducing your stress levels. Work on saying no as "often as" you say yes. As much as you want to be productive, come to terms that you cannot do every-thing at once. It would be best if you let some things go. If possible, reduce your commitments. A clearer mind equals a more peaceful home.

Thirdly, get a gratitude journal. Every night, write down what you are happy about (especially about your child). It could be as little as how much sleep you got that day to as much as how joyful your child was during the day.

Lastly, create a schedule for physical exercise and diet. Since both activities help reduce your stress levels, you will develop a less angry mind in the long run.

2

MY CHILD WON'T LISTEN!

Anger usually stems from triggers, and as a parent sometimes your child's challenging behavior may trigger you to get angry. Since you are predisposed to think you are the one who shapes your child's life, it is easy to become angry when you deal with little, naughty behaviors.

This chapter will shift the focus from you to your child. Learning how to help them with their challenging behaviors goes a long way in becoming a calm parent and bringing up a happy child.

It's time to learn how your little one thinks. Let's look at some examples of the different kinds of anger-wrecking behaviors children exhibit. Which boxes does your child tick?

THE TANTRUM THROWER

Chances are you've been on the receiving end of a tantrum or two (or ten). Tantrums are a normal part of toddlerhood, and usually happen when they are tired, hungry, or frustrated. While they can be frustrating (and even embarrassing) for parents, tantrums are actually a sign that your toddler is developing normally. As they get frustrated and still lack the words to convey their feelings, it often is expressed as tantrums. Take a breath. Usually, this is a developmental stage that they will eventually outgrow. Still, before they learn patience and become better managers of their emotions, this character could irk you.

For instance, our son Hans, would throw tantrums whenever he didn't have things go his way. One day, we were walking past a toy shop, and he spotted a toy he wanted on the window. Unfortunately, we were running late to his doctor appointment and couldn't stop at that exact moment. As you would imagine, we got a huge tantrum show right in the middle of a busy walkway.

We thought it was only our child who did this until we discovered how prevalent tantrums are among toddlers, specifically two-year-old's. This is the age when language is starting to develop, so they tend to respond to frustration and anger with tantrums as they do not know how to communicate their feelings yet.

So, when your child is stomping, crying, biting, screaming, hitting, and throwing things, as crazy as it may sound, they are having a much tougher time than you think. At this stage it's important to practice staying calm (remember, it starts with you). Yelling and losing your cool will only make the situation worse. Again, count to 10 in your head and try to identify the cause of the tantrum. Is your child tired, hungry, or thirsty? If so, addressing those needs may help to stop the tantrum. If all else fails, try to distract your child with a tree leaf, a stuffed animal, or a bug.

As your child grows older, the rate of tantrums should reduce. However, you cannot wait for more years before dealing with it, right? We couldn't either. So, we underwent some research, and here are some methods that helped us deal with our kid's tantrums:

- If your toddler is throwing a tantrum in an area that risks getting hurt or hurting others, move your child to a quieter place.
- Allow your child to experience the tantrum. Acknowledge your toddler's feelings. Let them know that it's okay to feel angry and that you

understand they are going through a tough time.

- Use nature or take a walk as a distraction. Doing this when the tantrum is at its initial stage will be best.
- Try making a silly joke or face. Introducing humor while your child is throwing a tantrum might work to reduce the angry feelings.
- Once the tantrum subsides, have a conversation. Help your toddler identify the source of their anger. Restate repeatedly that it is normal to have such feelings. Ask them what made them feel that way, while talking to them in a low-pitched voice.

Again, tantrums are your child's way of expressing themselves. To help them develop a better way of communicating their frustrations, you want to teach them good anger management skills as early as toddler-hood. Here's tips on how you can do so:

- Begin by controlling your outbursts. Since your child models you, be a good model by gently dealing with your anger. Hence, the importance of practicing how to stay patient during their tantrum trials.

- Whenever your child does something you like, positively reinforce your child's action by acknowledging it. "I'm so happy you chose your clothes all by yourself!"
- Be clear on the difference between their feelings and their actions. Encourage your toddler to express their anger in a positive way. When communicating with your child after a tantrum, explain that when they may feel a certain way, there are ways to express it differently. You could say, "I understand you had a really hard time today my love, next time you have these same feelings you can try to say, I'm really angry because…"

With a little patience and some trial and error, you'll be able to get through those tantrums like a pro!

WHEN SHOULD YOU BE CONCERNED?

If you see that your toddler is struggling to cope with their anger or the tantrums last for extended periods of time, it's important to seek professional help. A therapist can provide specific guidance and support to both you and your toddler as you work through these emotions together.

▷ The one with irrational behaviors

"I want the green cup!"

"I don't want to go to bed now!"

"I don't want to put on pants today!"

Sounds familiar? Why should these even be an argument? Since you are the parent, you should be the one making the rules, right?

I bet your child thinks otherwise.

At this developmental stage, toddlers are becoming ever aware of their emotions, exploring their independence, and testing limits. This drives them to want to make their own decisions.

So, to show a display of their abilities, they decide to make decisions seemingly opposite to yours. While you may consider this irrational, it is entirely normal.

Among the many things that influence a child's behavior, the child's emotions are at the very core. The part of the brain that deals with logic and self-regulation doesn't begin developing until age 4-5. Hence, toddlers are driven by emotion- what they want, not what we believe is best for them.

See this stage as an opportunity to teach your child good coping behaviors. As a parent, there are steps you can take to deal with your child's irrational behavior:

- **Be empathic.** You don't want to be one of those parents who shut out their kids whenever they demand something. A gift embedded in every human is the power of choice. We all decide what we want- including your child. Although in your eyes it might not be the best choice at the moment, you want to show that you understand the point your child's trying to raise and that you are on their team. For instance, if you are having trouble convincing your toddler to go to bed, you could say: "I know you don't want to go to bed now, but if you don't, you will wake up late and miss out on having fun with mom just before school tomorrow."
- **Be the one in control.** The worst thing you could do is engage in a power tussle with your child. Just like when your child is throwing a tantrum, be calm. Talk calmly. An upset parent versus an upset child is the perfect formula for guilt.
- **Give your child the power of choice.** Lay before your toddler a couple of options and wait

for a choice. This gives your child a sense of control and allows them to make their own decisions within the limits you set. For example, you could ask, "Do you want to wear the blue shirt or the green shirt?" or "Would you like to have a banana or an apple for a snack?" If your toddler is having difficulty deciding, you can offer a third option. Remember that toddlers feel a sense of control and accomplishment when they are able to make their own choices within the limits you set. Parents can use this technique to avoid power struggles and help their toddlers feel a sense of control and accomplishment.

THE EVER-CRYING TODDLER

You may feel like you are losing your minds when your toddler is constantly crying. There are, however, some reasons why toddlers cry that may help you understand and cope with the situation.

One reason for all the waterworks may be that toddlers are still trying to communicate their needs. Again, they may not yet have the words to express what they want or how they are feeling, so crying may be their only means of communication.

Another common reason for toddler tears is frustration. Toddlers are learning about the world and their place in it, and they can get frustrated when things don't go the way they want. They may cry when they can't figure out how to do something or when they are unable to communicate what they want.

Toddlers may also cry when they are tired, hungry, or in pain. These are all basic needs that need to be met in order for a toddler to feel comfortable and happy.

Additionally, some toddlers simply cry because they are overwhelmed by their emotions. They may be feeling sad, scared, or angry and not know how to express those feelings in any other way.

While it can be frustrating and exhausting to deal with a crying toddler, you should keep in mind that it is often a normal part of development.

That said, should you discourage crying as a parent?

No!

Science shows that some of the benefits include:

- Crying helps reduce physical stress. Conversely, suppressing tears increases stress levels.
- Crying reduces blood pressure and pulse rates.

- Crying helps eliminate certain toxins in your body that could build-up due to emotional turmoil, such as a frustrating day.

So, when does crying become excessive?

Since crying is okay, it is acceptable for your child to cry. However, it is not good for your child to believe bursting open a tear gland is a blank cheque to get something. Again, if your child is always crying to get your attention, don't **always** give in (if it is safe not to do so). The keyword is "always." On most occasions, you should give your child attention. However, not doing so every time would teach them a crucial life skill- people don't always get everything they want.

What do you do when your child is crying?

- Confirm your child is not in any physical pain.
- Try to understand why your child is crying. Is your child Hungry, Angry, Lonely, or Tired? Is your child HALT?
- Stay close. You want your child to know that you are still there. This might mean giving your baby a soothing hug, holding their palms, or maintaining eye contact for an extended period.
- Try to distract your toddler with something, perhaps, a toy or looking out the window.

- If possible, leave the present environment and go for a walk. Nature often seems to have a way of doing the trick with children.

A GUIDE FOR PARENTS

Your job as a parent is to help your toddler navigate this crucial developmental period. This will not only be important for your sanity in the long run, but also essential for who your child becomes tomorrow. Honestly, yes, it will take some effort. Yes, your child is dealing with lots of emotions. And, yes, we know exactly what you are going through. But no, it doesn't have to be difficult. There are simple things you do to guide your child through this period.

Be open about your feelings. When you feel frustrated, say it. When you feel happy, voice it. When you feel angry, tell them. Your child might recognize the emotions but lack the words to communicate them. Once you turn this into a habit, you will solve a significant problem. What is a better way of teaching than showing?

Use visual aid to help waiting become easier. This is something we learned through months of practice. Start a timer if you want your child to wait for 10 minutes before the food becomes ready. If you want your child to get dressed fast, point at the clock. Visual aids help your child become optimistic that they don't have to wait forever!

Help your child practice self-control. Many games require the participant to take turns. For instance, rolling a ball back and forth. These kinds of games offer a great avenue to teach your child a vital lesson: things won't always be in your kid's control; however, your kid's reaction is always within control.

Encourage your child's independence. This can be as simple as letting your child pick out their own clothes or helping them pour their own milk. As they get older, you can give them more responsibility around the house, such as setting the table or feeding the pets.

Compliment your child. This is important for their self-esteem. When they do something well, make sure to let them know. It doesn't matter if it's something small, such as putting away their toys or sharing with a friend. What matters is that you are acknowledging their effort and letting them know that you are proud of them.

When we decided to go this route, we had so much digging to do, and what kept us going was the goal of a better tomorrow for our children. Little did we know that not only were we making the toddler years easier for our children, and also parenthood enjoying for us. The goal of understanding how to deal with the behaviors your child presents is not only for their development, at the same time you are building your emotional "muscles". So, when you see your child throwing a tantrum or crying as loud as a siren, your instant reaction won't be to scream but rather help them overcome their phase like a pro!

INTERACTIVE ELEMENT- SUMMARY

- Tantrums are normal. It's a crucial time for development, and you play a vital role in helping your child learn healthy coping skills.
- It starts with you. Your child will model your behavior. Express your feelings, so your child can also learn how to express themselves in a positive manner.
- Give your toddler the power of choice. Lay down options before your child and wait for a choice. This gives your child a sense of control and allows them to make their own decisions within the limits you set.
- Crying is okay. Don't discourage your toddler from crying, but don't also allow them to get everything through crying. However, remember to make sure that your child's

safety comes first. Pick your battles
appropriately.

- The second step to managing your anger is
  recognizing your toddler's present stage and
  learning how to guide them through it.
- The phase of a toddler's life is one full of new
  experiences and emotions. Your toddler's brain
  is about 80 percent developed by the age of
  three. That means they're learning and growing
  at an incredible rate! Be empathetic.

In the next chapter, you'll learn how to work on your
parenting style.

3

WHAT'S YOUR STYLE?

What's your parenting style?

Does that question sound familiar? When did you first hear about the term "parenting style?" An online quiz? A magazine? On the parents' forum?

Regardless of where you heard of it, chances are you didn't pay much attention to it. And that's okay, given that you didn't get a "how to parent successfully" manual alongside your child.

Although it is a popular term, many people do not understand how impactful our parenting style is on our children. It affects their personality, physical health, emotional health, and mental health. Therefore, learning the style you use and finding ways to improve its effectiveness not only makes you an exceptional parent, but it also sets the tone for your child's success in life.

Luckily, the effects of certain parenting styles aren't just one-sided. However, it is essential to understand different parenting styles, and how they can impact a child's development.

Since our definition of a great parent vastly differs, you can learn to pick up traits from the styles you believe would help you create the parenthood of your dreams.

PARENTING STYLES

The definition of a parenting style is the way in which parents interact with their children. This interaction reflects the values and beliefs of the parents, as well as their own experiences with being parented. To determine the parenting style of an individual, a lot of factors are put into consideration, including, but not limited to:

- The parent's action towards the child (Does the parent make sacrifices for the child?)
- The parent's attitude towards the child (Is the parent warm and empathic?)

- The degree of demands a parent place on the child (What expectations does the parent have towards the child?)
- How much the parent responds to the needs of the child (Quick or lackadaisical)
- The communication style used by the parent (Does the parent tear the house down with yells, or is the parent as gentle as a dove?)
- The level of self-control exhibited by the parent

These can be placed into three categories: how parents exhibit love towards their children, how parents deal with their kids' desires and needs, and how parents exercise their authority over their children.

However, one thing is for sure: the communication style used by a parent is highly influenced by the way they were raised. When the concept was first introduced in the 1960s by a lady named Diana Baumrind, she grouped parents into four categories:

- Authoritative parenting
- Authoritarian parenting
- Permissive parenting
- Uninvolved/neglectful parenting

After further digging into the science of family socialization, researchers came up with three more categories:

- Free-range parenting
- Helicopter parenting
- Attachment parenting

In this chapter, we will be diving deep into what each of these parenting styles entails, examples of the styles, and the pros & cons of each style.

Come along.

AUTHORITATIVE PARENTING

▷ **What it means and common traits**

Authoritative parenting is characterized by high demands on your child while having a high level of empathic understanding. So, while an authoritative parent will be warm and encourage independence in their child, these parents consistently enforce boundaries and dish out an educated measure of discipline when necessary.

Usually, these kinds of parents do not demand respect- they earn it. They raise their kids with both love and discipline- balancing both on the parenting scale. Although open communication is encouraged, clear boundaries (that cannot be crossed) are set. When they have a point to make, authoritative parents will use explanations and mutual reasoning as their toolkit rather than threats, yells, and punishments. The middle ground between firm and fair is where an authoritative parent stands.

▷ **Examples of authoritative parenting**

Some practical applications of authoritative parenting include:

- If a child starts throwing toys, instead of shouting and yelling, an authoritative parent will take time to explain the consequences of doing so: such as others may get injured. Then, the parent lays out the consequences of doing so again. For instance, if the child throws the toy again after the parent has explained the consequences, the parent might take the toy away and say to the child, "it seems as you are not ready to play with this toy. I will put it away and you can try again later."
- Imagine a toddler being angry. In the early stages of a child's life, emotions are a foreign concept; they are difficult for a toddler to fully understand. Authoritative parents have come to understand this and acknowledge the child's feelings. They validate their child's emotions by

using phrases like "It looks like you are upset because you don't want to leave the park yet. But it's time to go home, you can either walk to the car or hop like a bunny to the car." This demonstrates to the child that their feelings are validated and respected yet shifting their focus from being upset to having the independence to make a choice of hoping or walking to the car.

▷ Advantages of authoritative parenting

A study suggests that children with authoritative parents tend to be more self-confident and have higher self-esteem. This is linked to the fact that authoritative parents create an atmosphere where it is easy for their children to air their opinions and views about decisions involving them. Children in such homes feel safe and secure.

Again, several studies have found that children in such homes displayed to be emotionally intelligent. One crucial trait found in these parents are they help children through obstacles rather than completely removing the obstacles for them. Over time, children develop better-coping skills to deal with emotions, such as anger, fear, and frustration.

Another study from Fairleigh Dickinson University indicates that children with authoritative parents tend to do better academically. This could point to the fact that authoritative parents are often invested in their children's lives, setting reasonable goals for their children from a young age.

As you would expect, in a home where boundaries and rules are set and practiced, a likely consequence will be positive behaviors. Look at it from this angle: before going against the rules, the children are aware of the consequences. They are sure their parents won't be lenient enough to let them off the hook. More so, these children understand why their parents set the rules in the first place. So, it is easier to follow the rules than rebel against it. This is known as **inductive discipline**- a parental disciplinary method that involves using reasoning (induction) to explain parent's actions, values, and disciplinary approaches.

Lastly, since effective communication is the bedrock in such homes, children with authoritative parents often develop good communication and social skills.

▷ **Disadvantages of authoritative parenting?**

As an authoritative parent, it may take a lot of patience and will-power to implement boundaries that you can consistently follow through with. If you do not implement them gradually, it puts a lot of pressure on parents and becomes a burdensome.

Additionally, if this type of parenting is taken to the extreme, you might end up having a rule for every single thing in your house. The home should be a place where both you and your children enjoy. However, in a situation where you've got a rule staring at you in whatever direction you turn, your home will become a dreaded place (something you do not wish for). The way out of this is to ensure there is a balance between rules and fun. If a behavior isn't detrimental to your toddler's development in the long run, allow "King Fun" to rule to the day!

AUTHORITARIAN PARENTING

▷ **What it means and common traits**

This is the strictest form of parenting which often takes the "traditional approach" to raising children. Parents who use this style are often unresponsive to their children's needs and emotions. When boundaries are crossed, punishments are routed out without hesitation. In an authoritarian home, it isn't uncommon to hear the walls vibrating due to the yells constantly dished out by the parents.

While the children's failures are dealt with instantly, the children's achievements are often ignored and, if not so, celebrated minimally.

Are you an authoritarian parent? Here are some common traits of such parents:

- They have an insane level of expectations for their kids.
- They deal with misbehavior impatiently.
- They spend little or no time thinking about the child's perspective when making decisions and setting rules.
- They don't give their children the freedom to make choices, as they often believe they know better and should therefore be the one fully in charge.
- They are characterized by being insensitive to their kid's emotions. In such homes, there is a general lack of empathy.
- They show little or no warmth when disciplining their children. When instilling morals, the feelings of the children are not considered. Often, they result in the use of shaming as a way of getting their children to obey their rules.

▷ **Authoritarian parenting in action**

Let's refer back to our example of a child who throws toys, this time, probably, at a sibling. While an authoritative parent would explain the consequences of doing so and set rules to minimize future occurrences, authoritarian parents' immediate reaction will be to yell at their children. The difference is often a lack of patience and communication.

▷ Are there advantages of authoritarian parenting?

While it may no longer be the most popular parenting style, there are some advantages to authoritarian parenting. For one, this style of parenting can result in well-behaved children. Toddlerhood is often a challenging time for parents, but those who utilize an authoritarian parenting style may find that their toddler is more obedient and compliant, even if its due to the fear of punishment.

Additionally, this type of parenting can instill a strong sense of discipline, toughness, and safety in children. This can be beneficial later in life when children face more challenges and opportunities to make poor choices. Authoritarian parenting may not be right for everyone, but it can certainly have its benefits.

▷ Disadvantages of authoritarian parenting

Children raised by authoritarian parents usually have low self-esteem. This is majorly because these parents usually use techniques that suppresses the child's development by providing them with little opportunity to practice decision making. In turn, the children grow up doubting their worth and potential.

Even though authoritarian parenting may produce less toddler tantrums, it is not because the child is maturing. It tends to stifle a child's creativity and independence, causing the child to feel anxious or insecure. If taken to the extreme, children that grow in these types of homes are prone to have difficulty developing healthy social relationships.

This type of parent's will brag about their children's "impeccable" well-behavior. However, studies have found that even though in the short term such parents might achieve their goal of getting the children to live by their rules, in the long-term, it increases a child's risk of developing mental health problems, such as anxiety or depression and lead them to feeling resentful or rebellious.

"Because I said so!", rules these types of homes.

PERMISSIVE PARENTING

This kind of parenting generally does not enforce many rules or boundaries and permits their children do whatever they want. While the parents control the game in an authoritarian home, it is the kids who call the shots in a permissive home. There is barely any confrontation or discipline when the children display behaviors that go against usual moral standards.

"Kids will be kids" is the over-stated phrase among permissive parents. Being very lenient, their level of expectations from their children is relatively low, and therefore, they may not learn how to behave properly or control their impulses.

Common traits among permissive parents include:

- They have few rules and expect barely any level of maturity from their children.
- They emphasize their children's freedom while leaving out a sense of responsibility.
- They rarely discipline their children and often use rewards such as toys and sweets to get them to do certain things.

▷ **Example of permissive parenting**

If their toddler throws a temper tantrum when they tell them that it is nap time, but child doesn't want to stop playing at that moment, instead of enforcing the nap time for the benefit of their child, in a desire to stop the tantrum quickly, permissive parents will allow their child to skip naptime for playtime. Again, after all, "kids will be kids."

▷ **Effects of permissive parenting**

We all love freedom. No one, including your two-year-old, wants to be kept in check by rules. Since permissive parents go down this lane, toddlers that grow up in this home praise their upbringing when they become older. They brag about their parents being understanding and loving.

However, the result of permissive parenting might not be the best for children in the long run. After extensive research, psychologists concluded that this overly relaxed form of parenting could lead to several adverse outcomes.

Here are some of these outcomes:

- The children tend to be low achievers in areas of interest. Since their parents fail to have grounded expectations that their kids should strive to meet, they may be less academically motivated than their peers.
- These kids show a lack of emotional stability when things don't go their way outside their home. The freedom they were exposed to as a child makes them believe they should have the final say regarding any matter, which, unfortunately, is not how the world works.

- The lack of proper structure and rules in their home gives them an avenue to mismanage their time and develop poor habits. For instance, spending the entire day watching television. This manifests into a lack in motor-skill development, focus, physical health, and self-discipline.

So, while permissive parenting can have its benefits, such as having a child praise their loving and chill upbringing, it's important to be aware of the potential downsides if you are too laxed in this parenting style.

UNINVOLVED PARENTING

Also known as neglectful parenting, uninvolved parenting is characterized by parents who show little or no responsiveness to the child's needs aside from the basic necessities such as food, clothing, and shelter. Their children grow up lacking the appropriate love and affection, as on the warmth scale, these parents score very low.

Asides from that, uninvolved parents do not demand much either. They are generally less involved with their child's life and provide little guidance or support. This can lead to children feeling neglected or unimportant.

If for any reason this speaks to you, before judging yourself, you must understand that this form of parenting isn't a one-time thing. As parents, we've all had moments where we sacrifice paying attention to our children for minutes of solitude and "peace." If you've done so, you aren't an uninvolved parent. This form of parenting refers to an ongoing pattern of emotional distancing between the parent and the child.

Some common characteristics of uninvolved parents include:

- When making decisions, the children are never taken into consideration.
- Everything ranks above spending quality time with their children. These parents prioritize everything else and ignore how vital spending time with their children is.
- Absence of warmth, love, attention, and lack of emotional bonding between the child and the parent is evident in the relationship.
- Unless the child's behavior directly impacts them, these parents fail to engage in disciplinary measure to correct the child. And it's rarely in a positive manner.
- They show little or no support during the children's activities.

While it might be easy to point fingers at parents stuck in this form of parenting, we should not do so. Notice we used the word "stuck." That's because for many of these parents it's psychologically unintentional on their part. Parents who were raised by neglectful parents often find themselves repeating similar patterns when raising their children. Also, these parents tend to get caught up in their busy lives. They find it difficult to balance work and family life, with work taking a more significant percentage of their time.

For emphasis's sake, skipping your family game night just because you had a pile of work in the office to attend to doesn't automatically slam the "uninvolved" parent title on you. If you spend your free time with your children and even ensure they are cared for when you are not around, you are not a neglectful parent. (Did we hear a sigh of relief?)

▷ **Example of neglectful parenting**

Parent often chooses to stay late at work, and repeatedly dismisses their children's plea for attention. As their child excitedly jump on their laps when they get home, uninvolved parents will consistently display indifference towards the child even if it's for a few minutes before their bedtime. They may greet the child but quickly will put them down and go about their evening to-do list.

This is just one example of the many ways in which neglectful parenting can have a devastating effect on a child.

▷ **Effects of uninvolved parenting**

Children raised in this type of home may lean towards self-reliance. Although you could consider this a good trait, neglectful parenting can lead to serious consequences for the child including developmental delays, emotional problems, and behavioral issues, as the lack of an emotional connection with their parents results in low self-esteem and an emotional craving in future relationships that should have been satisfied by their parents as early as in toddlerhood.

Again, the unfulfilled love, bond, and attention, makes it difficult for these children to develop into well-rounded kids. These children often have a hard time being in social gatherings and excelling in school. Additionally, research shows that children raised by an uninvolved parent have shown to have an increased risk of substance abuse.

Now, don't go too hard on yourself if you feel you're an uninvolved parent. You are reading this book; you already have taken a huge step forward. While it is impossible to change the past, the future is still within your reach. If neglectful parents raised you, you might want to also seek therapy. Getting help does not mean you failed, it means you want to succeed. Let the past go. Today is a new day, and today is the best day to change your future and your child's future.

FREE-RANGE PARENTING

Free-range parenting finds its home somewhere between permissive parenting and neglectful parenting. In such homes, children are allowed to engage in independent activities and, if necessary, experience firsthand the consequences of their actions. It is a kind of parenting that aims at ensuring children grow up with the life-coping skills needed to handle the challenges they may encounter as an adult.

However, there seems to be a thin line between free-range parenting and neglectful parenting. It isn't always clear when a child is old enough to handle specific responsibilities. Coupled with the fact that what might be acceptable in one place and considered neglect in another, free-range parenting has generated a lot of debates over the years.

According to a Washington Post article, a child in a neighborhood park is more likely to be hit by lightning than to experience abduction. Yet, opposing parents still don't even support the idea of giving a toddler the freedom to explore the neighborhood park while they watch from afar. They believe toddlers need close attention constantly. On the other hand, supporting parents believe that free-range parenting is not being neglectful but allowing children to learn from their mistakes and conquer their world freely. To bring this home, free-range parenting with toddlers could mean allowing them to explore new environments without consistently helping, hovering over, or interrupting them.

Some common traits of free-range parents include:

- They believe the more age-appropriate risks a toddler experiences, the stronger they grow up to be physically and mentally. This means letting their toddler ride the slide alone, instead of holding their hands while they do it.
- They allow their toddlers to earn their independence gradually. Instead of allowing their kids off the hook at once, these parents would instead grant increased freedom and responsibility as they notice their child matures.
- They allow their toddlers to try new things. They don't parent out of fear but give their child the liberty to live their childhood like an adventure, exploring new opportunities.

- Free-range parents do not overly supervise every activity their toddlers are engaged in. However, there is still some level of parental guidance and advice.

If you are not familiar with this style of parenting it can be very tricky to understand it, so let's look at a famous example to shine more light on it.

▷ **Example of free-range parenting**

Lenore Skenanzy, a New York columnist, made headlines when she wrote an article titled "Why I Let My 9-Year-Old Ride the Subway Alone." The story gained national attention as people weighed in on her decision.

Skenanzy is clear that she made sure her son was able to read the subway map, and she gave him money in the event he needed it. But critics still argued her decision bordered on child neglect. Skenanzy started a movement to encourage parents to stop being helicopter parents. She warned about the dangers of overprotecting children.

Her story is an example of free-range parenting, a parenting style that advocates giving children more independence and responsibility. Referring back to toddlers in the park, many parents are hesitant to let their toddlers roam too far from them, but free-range parents find it important to give them the opportunity to explore. They believe that allowing your toddler to play independently, within your distant supervision, can help them develop important life skills.

▷ **Effects of free-range parenting**

Giving your toddler the liberty to safely explore their environments will help them become self-reliant, independent, and resourceful over time. It will also instill in their decision-making and problem-solving skills, which are crucial for success in today's world.

Although there are risks your child can get hurt during their little exploits, the chances may not be as high as you think. However, if you're considering a free-range parenting approach, it's important to do your research, ensure you are keeping it age appropriate, and that you're comfortable with it. If done correctly, free-range parenting can be a great way to raise independent, resilient, and responsible kids.

HELICOPTER PARENTING

They are parents characterized by overinvolvement and overprotection of children. It is also known as "hover parenting". They typically are those parents who are highly involved in their child's life and make decisions for them, rather than letting the child make decisions for themselves. This parenting style is often criticized for creating a generation of entitled, spoiled children who are not able to handle adversity or setbacks.

There are a few different types of helicopter parents. The first type is the micro-manager. Micro-managers are those who try to control every aspect of their child's life. They make decisions for their children and often do not allow them to experience anything on their own.

The second type of helicopter parent is the enabler. Enablers are those who do not want their children to experience any hardship or disappointment. They often give their children everything they want and do not allow them to experience anything negative.

The third type of helicopter parent is the rescuer. Rescuers are those who always step in to help their children when they are in a difficult situation. They do not allow their children to experience any challenges or problems.

▷ **Example of helicopter parenting**

While taking a stroll around the neighborhood lake with their toddler, helicopter parents will love to hold their child's hand to ensure they don't fall down and scrapes a knee for instance. They watch their child's every step as they can't bear the thought of their child experience any pain or discomfort.

▷ Effects of helicopter parenting- the two sides of the coin.

There is a lot of research that has been conducted on helicopter parenting and its effects. Some studies have found that helicopter parenting can lead to children who are less independent and more reliant on their parents. Other studies have found that helicopter parenting can lead to children who are more anxious and stressed.

While helicopter parents' intentions are good and promote the child's safety, always stepping in during a crisis will deprive your child of the privilege to learn crucial problem-solving skills.

Children of helicopter parents have a higher tendency of becoming highly dependent on their parents, which isn't the best trait for a child. Studies show that it is best to train your child to make good decisions without so much of your assistance. But how would this be possible if they were not given a chance to make decisions?

The normal parent-child relationship gives space for children to opt for what suits them best. Ask any child- they want freedom. Although the intentions of a helicopter parent are something every parent should have, these parents should take caution to make their actions moderate.

The craving for independence locked away within the children of such parents might cause these children to detest their parents rather than want them as they get older. The goal of parenting should be to guide and prepare your toddler for the future. Your toddler will need to make critical decisions sooner than later.

As a parent, in any area of your child's life, it is best for children when they grow up choosing guidance instead of dependence. Children with strong communication skills as well as effective decision-making, will grow into complete, self-confident, and emotionally healthy humans.

ATTACHMENT PARENTING

Rather than a form of parenting, attachment parenting can be a mentality some parents have towards their children. Here, parents engage in a child-centric approach that aims at connecting with their children on a deep emotional level. The goal is to set the stage for secure relationships later in the child's life by increasing the parent-child bond presently. This way, the children grow to form healthy, emotional connections later in life.

Attachment parenting can be characterized by certain traits, some of which are:

- The urge to make informed decisions, leading the parents to seek out medical information on the subject matter. The goal is to pick options that would foster emotional connections with the child.
- These parents would rather opt for gentle disciplinary approaches than spanking and sarcasm when correcting the child.
- They endeavor to respond to the child's needs quickly. Needs such as affection, nutrition and sleep are at the top of their list.
- They are careful when choosing caregivers, as their values and that of the caregiver must align to promote harmony.
- They take time out to care for themselves as well. They understand that to give their child the best care, they must be healthy and fully energized themselves.
- They are known for advocating for breastfeeding, as they believe it's an essential bond as well as it develops the child's healthy emotional, physical, and mental development.
- They would rather opt for slings and front carriers ahead of strollers and car seat carriers

because they place importance on having as much physical contact with their child as possible.

- They are involved in co-sleeping, which refers to sleeping within the arm's reach of the baby.

▷ **Example of attachment parenting**

If their toddler just had a nightmare and wants to sleep in bed with them. They gladly create some space and allow it.

▷ **What is the difference between attachment parenting and helicopter parenting?**

Helicopter parenting refers to hovering over your child, envisioning the worst-case scenario for every situation, and causing them to be dependent on you. So, if you believe your toddler sliding at the park would cause your child to get injured, you will hold their hands all the way down the slide making sure they don't fall at the bottom. On the other hand, attachment parenting means being there for your child when they need you (and not when you think they do). It means giving your toddler the freedom to make their choices while still being a haven for them (and 100% present when they need you).

▷ Is attachment parenting good or bad?

Although one might conclude that attachment parenting causes the child to become overly dependent on their parents, science doesn't agree so. Science shows that children exposed to attachment parenting are emphatic and emotionally intelligent.

However, a common criticism against this type of parenting (which, in some ways, could be true) is that it could be mentally and physically draining for the parents. Unless these parents carefully plan their time, they could find themselves so consumed with the child's needs that they don't have time for other adult needed "things."

Additionally, the American Academy of Pediatrics disagrees with a common habit among these parents-co-sleeping with an infant. They believe that co-sleeping could lead to Sudden Infant Death Syndrome (SIDS). However, room-sharing is strongly encouraged.

Which parenting style do you follow?

Because the different parenting styles directly affect the child, evaluating where you are presently standing is the most effective way of moving forward. To do this, compare your demands with your responsiveness.

Your demands refer to the rules and boundaries you set, while your responsiveness talks about the amount of warmth and love you show your child.

Do you struggle with keeping to the consequences of the rules already laid down, although you shower your toddler with love and attention? Then, you might be a permissive parent.

Are you so strict that you don't see things as a child would see them when making key decisions in the home? Then, you might be leaning towards being an authoritarian.

Are you extremely over-involved in the activities of your child? Maybe you are a helicopter parent.

Are you consistently uninterested and barely involved in any activities with your child? You could be an uninvolved parent.

Do you want your child to have a taste of independence even as a toddler? Then, you could be a free-range parent.

Are you constantly craving physical contact with your child but still giving your toddler the liberty to make minor decisions? Hello, attached parent.

Have you struck a balance between being firm and fair simultaneously? Kudos, dear authoritative parent.

Which parenting style is most effective?

The truth is, when it comes to parenting, there isn't a one-size-fits-all approach. Parenting is more of an art than a science. Since we all have varying backgrounds as parents, our responsiveness, and the demands we place on our children will vastly differ. However, the best parents understand how to create a perfect mix of responsiveness and demand.

Children who grow up in such homes are seen to develop critical problem-solving skills and are better grounded. Unlike neglectful parents, these parents offer love and support to their children. Still, boundaries and rules are set in the home, and inductive discipline is engaged in (a crucial difference between authoritarian and authoritative parenting). While permissive parents allow their kids to do whatever they want to do, these parents interfere in their child's decision-making process with insights from adulthood experience.

Honestly, we can all agree toddlers are a special breed. They are old enough to be mobile; curious enough to explore their environment at this stage in their lives. However, they are still young enough to need constant supervision. Hence, this can make parenting a toddler a bit of a balancing act.

This means giving your toddler enough freedom to explore and learn from their mistakes while keeping them safe.

Again, since parenting doesn't have a one-size-fits-all approach, you need to find what works best for you. And honestly, this might take some trial and error to find the best path. But once you do, you've found the cheat code to parenting successfully; you set yourself up for an enriching (and enjoyable) parenting journey.

Although there are varying opinions on this subject (durhh...we are talking about parenting here), studies support that authoritative parenting was the more appropriate parenting style, as they were the parents who ticked most of the parenting boxes above.

INTERACTIVE ELEMENT- SUMMARY

The third step to managing your anger is figuring out the type of parenting style you currently use. Weight the pros and cons of it. Then, make tweaks to improve its effectiveness during your parenting journey.

There are as many children as the stars in the sky. And with this comes so many notable traits and features. Your toddler is unique in ways only you can fully articulate. Hence, your parenting style might not fit into one category.

And that's fine. It is possible to combine positive traits from other styles into your parenting. You could be an authoritarian and still learn how to treat your child more gracefully (like authoritative parents). However, a significant characteristic of effective parenting is prioritizing positive discipline rather than punishment in all you do. And you know what this means- fewer yells and more communication.

Lastly, don't be too controlling in a bid to create an excellent future for your child. Research suggests that your children will have the healthiest outcomes if you master the art of effective nurturing- guiding, not controlling.

In the next chapter, you will learn some positive parenting lessons to help you forge better connections with your toddler and become a more positive parent!

4

CONNECTING...5:1

Your toddler won't remain a toddler forever.

This little human that causes you to lose your cool and keep you on your toe's day and night, was once a cute, suckling infant and will soon become a preschooler, then a grade-schooler, a teen, and finally, an adult.

As your toddler encounter changes on their path of growth, your relationship with your little one will be ever evolving. Understanding how to foster positive connections with your toddler will strengthen your bond, make communication much easier, and help you manage your anger better.

YOUR TODDLER AND YOU- THE SECRET TO A HAPPY RELATIONSHIP

It's no secret that the toddler years can be challenging, both for parents and toddlers. But there are ways to make the toddler years easier and more enjoyable for both you and your toddler. The key is to understand your toddler's needs and how to best meet them.

Every home is different, and every child is unique, but the secret for building a happy and healthy relationship with your toddler lies in having a game plan. Winning will require creating a routine and sticking to it. Toddlers thrive on routine and predictability. Having a set schedule for meals, naps, and playtime will help your toddler feel secure and comfortable.

Therefore, its vital that you are consistent with your expectations and discipline. Toddlers need clear boundaries in order to feel safe. If you are consistent with your expectations and discipline, your toddler will know what to expect and behave accordingly.

Encourage independence. Toddlers are just beginning to learn how to do things on their own. Encourage their independence by letting them try new things, choosing their own clothes and giving them the space to explore.

Show patience and understanding. Toddlers are still learning and growing, and they will make mistakes. Show patience and understanding when your toddler makes a mistake and help them learn from it.

Express love and affection. Toddlers need lots of love and affection. Spend time cuddling, reading, and playing with your toddler. Let them know how much you love them every day. Enjoy this special time in your child's life and cherish the moments you share together.

Learn to be gracious with yourself. Parenting is not easy. You will make mistakes. That's what makes you human. But let's face the truth- it's easier said than done. We have three kids, we know!

We once had an issue with our first son Hans. When we had our second son Leo, he was about 2 years old. Just before he clocked two, it felt like he cried a lot more than he used to. At first, we didn't pay much attention to it, but shortly after it hit us, and we began to understand.

Since his mother had to deal with the responsibilities of being a new mother, our first son missed the attention he got. Of course, he didn't resent his new brother. Still, there was a part of him that wished he could have his mother's attention. In the mornings when he woke up earlier than us, it wasn't unusual to see him on our beds, trying to wake his mother up. But, since she had been up for most of the night (thanks to the obligations of motherhood), she could barely open her eyes.

Under normal circumstances, she would get up to greet him with all the love in the world and go play with him. He missed that. But she was too tired during this time. I had to fill her shoes. And, sure- it wasn't an easy one to fill.

There were times I had to keep our first son from hurting our newborn. He wanted to play with his new brother- turn his head and maybe sit on his back. Technically, that could lead to an injury. On one afternoon, he attempted to push his little brother off the couch and being stressed after a long week at work, I yelled at him to stop.

But he just wouldn't listen.

So, I went to where he was and hit his hands to grab his attention. I really didn't intend to cause him harm. He is my son. And I love him so much. But it was as if all of the stress in me came rushing out, giving more pressure on the little tap than I intended to give.

And there he was- my son crying his eyes out. And there I was too- feeling as the worst dad in the world.

Although I've had a couple of other similar experiences, I have learned to do three things whenever I lose my cool:

First, I consciously decide to forgive myself. And for each time I need to forgive myself, I remind myself that my emotions are real. My emotions are valid. That I'm human.

Secondly, I apologize to my child. I recognize that even though my child might have done something that set me off, my child is only a child. I also try to see the real reason my child did what he did. For instance, in this case my child only wanted to play with his brother. He had no clue he could hurt him. Recognizing this helps me see things from a different perspective, my child's perspective.

Thirdly, I challenge myself to five good acts. For every negative act I display, I counter it to five positive ones. This is something we did not know when we became parents but have put into practice since- the "magic" 5:1.

THE MAGIC OF THE 5:1 RATIO OF PARENTING IN CONNECTING WITH TODDLERS

Science approves of it. And now, parents are starting to realize more and more how impactful this principle is in connecting with their toddlers.

Initially, this experiment was carried out in the 1970s by two scientists who were determined to find out the difference between unhappy and happy couples. They asked some couples to solve their relationship conflict in 15 minutes while being taped.

After carefully reviewing the tapes and following up with the couples for nine years, the scientists discovered this specific ratio that makes love last. With this ratio, they could predict, with up to 90% accuracy, which couples would divorce.

The discovery was simple but crucial to the sustenance of a human relationship: a stable relationship has five more positive interactions for every negative interaction. In other words, if you have too few positive interactions to balance out the negative ones, you will most likely end up with an unhappy relationship.

And this rule isn't limited to just couples. It applies to all facets of human relationships: your co-workers, friends, family members, and even your children.

Let's face it: it is impossible to be positive all day long. There will be times you have negative interactions with your children. However, knowing to counter the effects of these bad interactions with good ones will help you make less mistakes and give you so much peace as a parent.

You will form a strong emotional connection with your child as you consistently engage this principle. And consequently, this tends to influence your child in a positive direction. The keyword is "**influence**."

So, how do you gain influence over your child? Simple: By building a respectful relationship with them. And you do this when you choose to counter every negative interaction with at least five positive ones. This leads to building a solid relation with your toddler and earning their respect from an early age.

Here are some examples of positive interactions you can have with your child:

▷ **Target at least 12 hugs daily**

Not just hugs; aim for as many physical contacts in a day. While assisting your toddler in dressing up, pet their hair. Before dropping your child off at the daycare, hold your child's hands. Just before hitting the bed, snuggle them in. Draw your child as close to your chest as much as possible and experience the warmth that comes with a genuine human, physical connection. And, not just you- your child will feel loved as well.

▷ Turn off technology when interacting with your child

Picture someone trying to do a thousand and one things while listening to you. How would you feel? Probably like an item that needs to be checked off their to-do list. While keeping up with at least five positive interactions, you could be caught in the web of attempting to do it because, well, it just needs to be ticked off your "being-a-good-parent" list. But that should not be so. Giving your total, undivided attention to your child could be one of the greatest gifts to your children.

▷ Show up

When they need you, be there! When your toddler is throwing tantrums, be emotionally present. When your toddler feels like playing, choose to live in the moment. Right there- let everything else fade away. You might be running on a tight deadline, but you always will be. There will always be a pressing challenge to solve. Sometimes, you need to tune down the noise and just show up because your toddler won't remain a toddler forever; your toddler's time also has a deadline, and it will expire in the blink of an eye.

▷ **Before transitions, connect!**

When they are deep into something, toddlers have difficulty transitioning to something else- especially something we want them to do. For instance, when toddlers play with their favorite toys, getting them to go for naps might be a daunting task. However, you can make it easier. When you want your toddler to do something important, look them in the eye and call out them by their name. Make prolonged eye contact and try to get your child giggling. This will act as the much-needed bridge to cause the transition.

▷ **Admit your mistakes**

Vulnerability is attractive to your toddler. It's the lifeblood of every relationship. When you come open with your children, you influence them to come open to you too. Everyone makes mistakes, and I'm sure you do too (except if you are some alien from Mars). And there will be times when you make mistakes when dealing with your child. You probably will yell at your child because of how stressed out you were at work. During these times, apologizing to your child will be the best thing to do. Not just for your child but also for you too.

▷ Make time for one-on-one time

This is more of a habit than something you do when you mess up. For at least 20 minutes every day, shut off the world and lean into your child wholly. During this period, you let your child take the lead. This might mean engaging in activities your child enjoys- which probably will involve playing with blankets and couch pillows. Sometimes, your toddler will babble on and on...but endeavor to remain present.

▷ Emotions are welcome here!

After a negative interaction, your toddler might have to handle a couple of emotions all at once. When this happens, acknowledge that your toddler can't display all these emotions well just yet. It might start with some tears and, sometimes, a tantrum display. Whatever it is, make it clear that your child doesn't have to hide the emotions.

▷ Share your childhood experiences

Scolding your child over a mistake is unavoidable sometimes. But you can flip the coin on this negative interaction and turn it into a positive one. Chances are you also did what you are scolding your child over when you were a kid. Tell stories of your childhood- how naughty you were and the consequences you faced. This will strengthen the feeling of connection your children have with you and remind them that you only have their best interests at heart.

▷ **Share a joke**

Family jokes are probably the most fun jokes. It keeps the family bonded, but it is also an excellent conflict resolution technique. After a negative interaction, use a joke to reduce the tension and draw your child closer. Knock, knock! It always seems to do the trick. As you make efforts to increase your positive interactions with your child, you should also attempt to reduce your negative interactions. Ramping up your positive interactions without minimizing the negatives is like pouring water into a leaking bucket- more effort, fewer results...

That said, here are some ways to avoid negative interactions with your toddler:

▷ **Keep the past behind you**

As parents, it is easy to judge our child's behavior from the lenses of the past. It is easy to compare the present behaviors of our toddlers with that of the past- especially if it is a recurring, negative behavior. However, doing this only makes your child feel humiliated and grieved over a mistake that cannot be erased. Instead, forget the past and focus on the present. As much as possible, don't remind your child of the past- especially if it is a negative one.

For example, if your toddler keeps throwing tantrums, instead of comparing their behavior to when they were younger and didn't tantrum as much, try to focus on the present and find ways to help them cope at the moment. Redirect their attention, offer them words of encouragement, hug them. This will be more beneficial for both you and your toddler in the long run.

▷ Don't scold, discuss

Discussion means tackling the problem while scolding means attacking your child. Fine- your toddler made a mistake. Your first reaction shouldn't be to show off your fiery temper. Instead, practice the counting and breathing techniques. Sit your child down and explain why such actions must not be repeated. Letting your toddler in on your thought process will make them aware of why the mistake shouldn't be repeated.

For example, "I know you didn't mean to hurt your brother but hitting is not a nice thing to do. It hurts people, and it makes them sad. We don't hit people, so how about you try to explain to your brother how you feel by using your words instead."

"If you hit him again, he will not want to play with you, and we will agree with his decision."

Remember, your toddler is always watching you, so it's essential to be a good role model. If you're constantly yelling and losing your temper, your toddler is more likely to do the same. Instead, try to stay calm and resolve conflicts peacefully. This will set an excellent example for your toddler and help them learn to cope with their own emotions.

▷ **Don't impose, guide.**

The best way to get someone do something is by getting them to want to do it. While imposition means forcefully pushing children to do something (even though it is for their good), guidance means showing your children the importance of the activity, allowing them to become genuinely interested in it, and then setting up a routine that gets the ball rolling.

For instance, if you want your toddler to eat healthy foods, don't just tell them to eat their vegetables. Instead, explain to them why eating healthy is important. Show them pictures of what unhealthy eating can do to the body. Let them help you cook meals so they can see how fun and delicious healthy food can be.

If you want your toddler to brush their teeth, don't just tell them to do it. Instead, explain to them why brushing their teeth is important. Show them pictures of what happens to teeth when they aren't brushed. Let them help you brush your teeth so they can see how fun and refreshing it is.

The bottom line is that if you want your toddler to do something, don't just impose it on them. Instead, take the time to guide them so they can understand why the activity is essential and how much fun it can be.

▷ **Don't shame your child. Like, never.**

When you shame your child for a mistake, you teach your child that you want them to appear perfect all the time (which is practically impossible). Plus, shaming your child- whether publicly or privately- could lead to depression and anxiety in kids.

For example, instead of saying, "You're so clumsy!" Try saying, "That was a hard fall. Are you okay?"

Or instead of saying, "I can't believe you wet the bed again! You're such a baby!" Try saying, "It sounds like you had a tough night; let's get you cleaned up."

It may sound cheesy but affirming your toddler with positive statements will help them feel better about themselves and it will also help build their self-esteem. So next time you're tempted to shame your toddler, resist the urge, and try one of the positive interactions instead.

The "magical" 5:1 changed our lives and became a crucial step in our everyday life. And there you have it, the fourth step towards anger management for parents with toddlers is working towards putting the "magical" 5:1 principle into practice. This will reduce negative interactions with your toddler while simultaneously increasing your positive interactions, strengthening your parent-child bond, making communication easier, and reducing how often you get angry.

INTERACTIVE ELEMENT- SUMMARY

- Create an interaction diary where you record your daily interactions with your child. First, this helps you become intentional about this system. Secondly, reviewing this journal will help you know specific areas you could work on.
- Don't be so caught up in the technology web that you neglect physical contact and one-on-one communication with your child. Your physical presence is vital; be intentional about it.

- The magic 5:1 principle shouldn't be restricted to dealing with your children. Apply it in other relationships you are involved in. Sit back and watch it work wonders on your connections with others.

Moving on, you will discover how to be your toddler's emotional coach!

5

COACHING TODDLERS

In the last chapter, we discussed balancing the negative interactions with more positive interactions with your child. Again, the "magic" 5:1 ratio. This chapter will explain why to be successful in life, it is crucial for children to develop emotional intelligence.

You may have heard the word "EQ." EQ stands for Emotional Quotient. Some people also call it Emotional Intelligence. Your EQ is the ability to understand, use and manage your emotions in ways that help you live optimally. Your emotional quotient will help you build stronger relationships with others and make informed decisions with your emotions in mind.

And guess what? Your Emotional Quotient is equally, if not more essential than your IQ to be successful in life.

We all know people who had the brains academically, but when it came to forging meaningful career relationships in the workspace, they sucked at it. Being bright alone will not make you fulfilled in life.

Therefore, if you want a life of happiness for your child- a life where your child is surrounded by people who are genuine, loving, and caring, a life where they understand how to build meaningful relationships, a life where your child is equipped to manage the ugly emotions humans have- then, it's important that you pay attention on developing emotional intelligence in your child.

The importance of a high EQ cannot be overestimated. A high EQ will rub off on your child's performance at school (when your child begins school), their physical health (by helping them handle high-stress levels), their mental health (by reducing the risk of anxiety and depression), and every single small or big decisions your child makes.

In other words, it really matters that your child's EQ is well developed.

Although there is an expected sequence your little one's growth follows through life, luckily, as a parent, you can intervene in this process and help make the milestones easier for them.

If this sounds like a lot of work, don't panic. As you will learn in this chapter, the stages of emotional development will clarify what you should be doing at each stage of your child's journey.

That said, let's dive right into the core of this chapter.

THE STAGES OF EMOTIONAL DEVELOPMENT

A German scientist known as Erik Erikson proposed these stages of emotional development. Erik was a scientist who specialized in child psychoanalysis. Most of his work was focused on how children develop the foundations of vital mental health.

Erik believed that there are eight stages of psychosocial development of any human- with the first stage beginning from birth and the last stage ending at death. At each stage, the individual would experience a psychosocial crisis.

Successful completion of each stage led to the acquisition of the fundamental virtues of that stage and hence, a healthier personality. On the other hand, failure to complete the stage successfully will lead to an unhealthy character.

That said, I will list out the eight stages. However, since this book is about toddlers, I will focus on the first two stages.

The eight stages of psychosocial development, alongside the fundamental virtue that will be developed upon successful completion of the stage, include:

Stage	Psychosocial crisis	Basic Virtue	Age
1.	Trust vs. Mistrust	Hope	0-1½
2.	Autonomy vs. Shame	Will	1½ - 3
3.	Initiative vs. Guilt	Purpose	3-5
4.	Industry vs. inferiority	Competency	5-12
5.	Identity vs. Role confusion	Fidelity	12-18
6.	Intimacy vs. Isolation	Love	18-40
7.	Generativity vs. Stagnation	Care	40-65
8.	Ego Integrity vs. Despair	Wisdom	65+

1. Trust vs. Mistrust

This is the first stage Erik proposed, and it lasts for the first 18 months after birth. This is the first psychosocial crisis children experience, and it revolves around the question: should the child trust the world and the people in it, or should the child mistrust the world? Children are uncertain of the world around them during this stage and depend on their primary caregiver for love and support.

The prerequisite for passing this stage successfully is if children receive predictable, reliable, and constant care from their primary caregiver. This will cause them to develop a sense of trust in the world and the people around them- leading to better relationships in the future.

On the other hand, if their needs are not met on a regular basis, anxiety, mistrust, and suspicion tend to be developed in the children at this stage.

The primary virtue in this stage is hope. If completed successfully, this stage gives the child confidence and trust that as new crises arise the people around them can be counted on as a significant source of support. On the contrary, failure to complete this stage will cause the child to develop mistrust and fear.

So, how do you (as a parent) help your child pass this stage successfully? Parents should be able to recognize their children's needs and act to fulfill those needs quickly. For instance, crying could mean that your child needs affection, comfort, a wonderful diaper change, or feeding. So, if an infant starts crying, don't wait until they are screaming out of the top of their lunges, meeting their needs as fast as possible will help a child pass this stage.

2. Autonomy vs. Shame

Before diving into this stage, allow us to tell you a bizarre, but true story.

The stage is set in 1967 when a chap called Martin Seligman conducted an experiment on helplessness and will. In this experiment, he divided a group of dogs into two groups and administered a couple of electric shocks to both groups. Please note that these electric shocks were not meant to harm the dogs. Think more of invisible dog fences today.

During the experiment, the first group was able to stop the shocks by completing a certain action, then they could move on to the next stage; however, regardless of whatever the second group did, the shocks wouldn't turn off on the next stage. Meaning they could not move on to the next stage.

Later on, Martin put both groups in another situation, whereby they could both turn off the shocks by carrying out simple steps.

Can you guess what the result was?

Yes, you are right. The second group of dogs felt helpless in the second experiment, even though they could turn off the shocks and just didn't move.

Why?

Because in the first experiment, they could not turn the shocks off no matter what they did.

I told this story because, in a way, it relates to the second stage of Erikson's model. Of course, there are no electric shocks involved. However, this is the stage children begin to explore the limits of their abilities. They are naturally inclined to move on to the next stage. They become aware that they are not an extension of their parents. Instead, they are independent beings with the ability to make certain decisions on their own.

Since you are the parent of a toddler, you would have experienced the various hallmarks of this stage. Toddlers will want to do things by themselves: choosing what to wear, trying to put on clothes by themselves, deciding whether to keep their clothes on, and becoming picky about what to have for dinner!

Erikson believed this stage is focused on developing a greater sense of self-control. At this stage, gaining an understanding of personal control over their choices is essential, as this will help them, as they grow older, to develop confidence in their abilities. Children who complete this stage are more likely to feel confident about their future decisions, while those who don't will most likely have to deal with feelings of inadequacy and self-doubt.

So, as a parent, what can you do to encourage success in this stage? As already stated, you will notice that your child will begin displaying a craving for independence. As a parent, your goal is to create an environment which is toddler failure tolerant and encouraging towards independence, not parent dependent. For instance, instead of putting their clothes on, support them by having a small number of clothing options to choose from in their closet that is at their eye level and easy to put on. Allow them to make their choice and put it on themselves until they succeed or ask for your help.

Another example of an important event in this stage is toilet training. As your child realizes that the toilet has to be visited when specific changes occur in the body, they will look for ways to communicate this with you. As a parent, you should proudly acknowledge your child when they speak up when the needs arise. A pat on the head or a word of affirmation will go a long way in helping your child in this phase.

On the other hand, since toilet training can be frustrating, you must consciously ensure you don't fill this period with voicing frustration or shaming. If you do, your child will develop a sense of shame and doubt.

And this extends beyond toilet training. For instance, children will communicate whether they want to play with toys or go outside. If you allow your child to explore these choices and make safe decisions, your child will develop a sense of autonomy. However, if you constantly make every decision for your child, your child will become doubtful.

A great way to help your child in this stage is to present choices A and B and let your child choose the best option. For instance, you could ask: "Do you want to do it now or in 20 minutes?" But still, remember to stand your ground on the non-negotiable, such as bedtime or school time. However, decisions such as the clothes to wear or the toys to play with can be made by your child.

The primary virtue at this stage is Will. If this stage is completed successfully, your child will develop the **Will** to make decisions personally.

That said, if there's one thing you have concluded from this chapter, it is that: your children's emotional intelligence is essential to be successful in life.

And, to make it as clear as possible, let's check out the steps every human undergoes when it comes to emotional development and how you can help your child foster growth at each point.

THE EMOTIONAL MILESTONES IN CHILDREN

Of course, the subject of emotions is not yet fully understood. However, there are three major steps regarding developing emotions the right way: noticing emotions, expressing emotions, and managing emotions.

▷ **Noticing emotions**

This occurs from birth to about when your child is a year old. No one knows for sure the innate emotions every child has. While some believe that the primary emotions are happiness, anger, and fear, others are of the opinion that every human is born with a lot more emotions than that. There's no way to know for sure since babies don't talk. But, from what we see- the cries and the giggles- we can conclude that they feel something. Or that babies have started noticing emotions.

How do you encourage growth in this stage?

First, don't discourage self-soothing. Activities like thumb-sucking are your child's first resort when it comes to regulating emotions. Although you might be tempted to jump in and save the day, don't discourage this.

Secondly, you need to recognize your children's needs and act to fulfill those needs quickly. We already mentioned this when explaining stage one of Erikson's theory. Every child is born with the desire to be loved, the need to be cared for. Whenever a child cries, consistently responding appropriately will create an environment of trust for them.

▷ **Expressing emotions**

This stage runs from age one to three, so most toddlers are in this stage. Honestly, this could be a very frustrating phase for parents. Here's where children begin expressing their emotions in new ways. Common ways include throwing tantrums and maybe, drawing what's on their mind. However, they experience complex emotions at this stage, and they've not yet deciphered the healthy ways to express them.

How can you foster growth in this stage?

Tantrums happen. It is normal for tantrums to happen. However, what matters is how you react to these tantrums. First, try not to lose your cool during these tantrums as much as possible. This means approaching them from an emotional point of view rather than a logical one. This is what we mean: If your child is throwing a tantrum over the fact that screen time is over, being logical will mean pointing out how absurd it is for your child to be angry even though you agreed on the screen time rules. On the other hand, approaching this from an emotional angle means being emphatic enough to validate your child's emotions while being firm on the rule. "I know you are angry that you cannot watch another episode of your favorite show, but remember what we agreed on the screen time rules?" Don't forget: Emotions are not logical.

Secondly, provide positive reinforcements regularly. It is easier to notice and "talk about" only the bad things your child does. But that will be counter-productive if that's all you do. Put this in your mind as you deal with your toddler: What you appreciate, appreciates. Hence, when children use their words and actions to explain how they feel, instead of kicks and screaming, affirming this act will count as a point for you. This doesn't mean parents should not correct children when they take the wrong turn; however, parents should balance their corrections with as many positive reinforcements.

Lastly, if children find it difficult to explain how they feel through words, parents should give them the words to use. For instance, telling your child to use the phrase "I'm angry!" instead of throwing a tantrum is a giant step towards the proper expression of emotions.

▷ Managing emotions

This phase lasts from age three to five, and most preschoolers fall within this bracket. In the last stages, children are primarily dependent on their parents when they feel certain emotions. However, children get exposed to a new social environment where they have to learn to share and play with others in this stage. Hence, it is essential that they develop personal coping skills for their emotions.

How can you foster growth in this stage?

First, validate as much as possible. Children at this stage might be tempted to think that they are the only ones who experience emotions like anger and frustration. You might also notice this happening with your toddler. Tell your kids it is normal to feel the way they do to counter this. Constantly saying statements like: "Your toy got damaged? I would feel angry too if I were in your shoes" will help your kid realize that emotions are not a bad thing. Plus, it prevents them from associating their emotions with shame.

Secondly, teach your kid coping mechanisms. And not just that; practice it in their presence too. For instance, if you feel angry, say it: "The car isn't coming on. I feel angry right now. I think I should take deep breaths. Can you join me in taking five deep breaths?" Doing something of this nature will help your kids associate certain emotions with corresponding coping mechanisms. Other coping mechanisms children find helpful include:

- Coloring.
- Retreating to a quiet place.
- Wrapping their arms around themselves and squeezing.
- Writing down what's bothering them and ripping the paper apart.

Remember, it is easier to teach your child something when you show it. Your kids will always emulate you. If you want to raise an emotionally intelligent kid, you must consciously teach your child these coping techniques. Helping your child through the emotional milestones is known as emotional coaching.

EMOTIONAL COACHING AND HOW TO DO IT LIKE A PRO

Emotional coaching involves teaching children how to recognize their emotions and the emotions of others, alongside helpful strategies to cope. Before going deeper into what emotional coaching is, it is necessary you understand what emotional coaching is not.

As grown-ups, it is easy to downplay our children's emotions to make them go away. However, merely sweeping your child's emotions under the rug won't make them go away. Using words like "just stop it" make children feel their reactions are wrong. Doing this is what psychologists call **Emotional Dismissing.**

And, you should know that emotional coaching is widely apart from emotional dismissing. The primary difference between these is that while emotional coaching involves acknowledging that your child's emotions are normal, emotional dismissing doesn't do so.

WHY IS EMOTIONAL COACHING NECESSARY?

Tons of research shows us the positive effects of emotional coaching and the harmful effects of emotional dismissing. Developing emotional regulatory skills will increase your child's chances of success in life. On the other hand, poor emotional management skills will increase the risk of your kid developing mental disorders such as depression and anxiety.

THE EMOTION-COACHING META-EMOTION PHILOSOPHY

Dr. John Gottman, an emotion development expert, proposed this philosophy. This philosophy states that parents who are good emotional coaches have five characteristics, namely:

- They are aware of their emotions and the emotions of their children.
- They turn emotional moments around for their good by using this intense period to teach their children regulatory skills rather than engaging in shaming.
- They occasionally see things from a child's perspective, helping them validate how their children feel.
- They verbally label the emotions their children express. "I see you are angry right now because..."
- They figure out the root cause of negative emotions, and through problem-solving skills, they deal with the situation that caused such emotions.

And you can use these five characteristics as the Dos of an emotional coach. Briefly, let's cover the don'ts of an emotional coach.

THE DON'TS OF AN EMOTIONAL COACH

- Emotional coaches do not invalidate their children's emotions.
- Emotional coaches don't expect instant changes. They learn to be patient as they

understand it's a journey, their children won't develop emotional regulatory skills overnight.

- Emotional coaches don't criticize or shame negative behaviors.
- Emotional coaches don't think short term. They think long term.

These are crucial things that we continue to remind ourselves daily. Being your child's coach is a lifetime decision that has a huge impact on your life and your child's life. Hence, choosing to become your child's emotional coach is the fifth step toward anger management for parents. How? When you help your toddler manage the new emerging emotions, they successfully ace their developing stages. As they do so, they become more emotionally intelligent and the more emotionally intelligent they are, the faster they mature. And guess what? The more mature they are, the more it reduces the number of situations that provokes you to anger.

INTERACTIVE ELEMENT- SUMMARY

- At this stage, a toddler needs a parent who creates an environment that promotes their independence. Parents should let their toddlers try to do something until they succeed and only step in when necessary.

- Don't criticize or shame your child's display of emotions. It's normal for toddlers not to know how to manage their emotions yet. Be patient with your child.
- Your children emotions matter, and how they develop emotional intelligence will have a crucial impact on their future, their life, their community, their parents lives and the world. Luckily, they have you as a coach. It's time to step up to the responsibility of training your children on how to manage their emotions well. Becoming your toddler's emotional coach will help your child become a well-grounded human and funny enough, help you enjoy parenthood more, because you will encounter a lot less stressful situation. Hence, this is the fifth step to anger management.

Since a major cause of anger is trying to correct your little one's negative behaviors, could it be that you may be doing it the wrong way? Is there a better way to discipline your child without resorting to flare-ups? Find out in the next chapter.

6

DISCIPLINE WITH LOVE

L et's play a game.

Are you in for it?

Okay, here we go: List out three to five things you love about parenting. For instance, watching your toddler jump up and down as you hand them the little toy, they wanted all week.

Done?

Now, list out the things you **don't** love about parenting. If you had your way, these are the stuff that you could pay to outsource. Don't worry; this is a safe space.

Done?

Okay! Do you know what our guess is? Somewhere near the top of your list is something to do with discipline.

And rightly so. How could it be that you are smiling with your child one minute, and the next, you are trying to stop them from engaging in recurrent behavior? It feels like an unending cycle that drives you bananas (often resulting in losing your shh... losing it). And that is what you don't want.

So, is it possible to discipline your toddler the right way?

We bet so. There's a term coined for such a kind of discipline: **Positive discipline.** And that's what we'll be covering in this chapter.

When children are exposed to positive discipline, they learn the value of being helpful, responsible, caring, and cooperative. Positive discipline encourages families to utilize skills such as agreement-making and problem-solving rather than yelling. This, in turn, promotes critical thinking, creativity, and responsibility- a bunch of skills you'd love embedded into your child.

TAKING THE POSITIVE PATH

If there's a positive path, there should be a negative path. And the difference between these two is what you choose to employ as a parent.

Let us explain.

Negative discipline means employing disciplinary methods such as spanking, yelling, or guilt-tripping whenever your child does something bad.

When you take the positive discipline path, you vow to explain things to your child. This includes explaining why they need to go to bed early and why they are not to take their clothes off in public. And you do this with a warm and friendly tone while maintaining your stand. In other words, positive discipline maintains the right balance between firm and loving.

But, regardless of how much you logically agree with this, this doesn't mean you won't feel frustrated sometimes. Even the Royal Family deals with it. Just YouTube: "Prince Louis throwing tantrum at Platinum Jubilee." Trust us, you will not be disappointed. However, what makes positive discipline effective is maintaining a positive and respective relationship with your child, whether you like their behavior or not.

And honestly, for anyone who has tried out parenting, that's easier said than done. We know. However, a great way to do this is to have a game plan, a pre-agreed consequences for actions. Doing this helps your children work through their feelings. Presenting your toddler with choices, explaining why they should take the good path, and dishing out the result of the path they choose (whether it be rewards or consequences) is called positive discipline.

IS POSITIVE DISCIPLINE EFFECTIVE?

When it comes to disciplining our children, we want what is best for them. We want to teach them right from wrong and help them grow into responsible, well-grounded adults. But is positive discipline always the most effective method?

Psychologists have found that negative discipline methods are usually ineffective in the long run. Not only that, but they can also lead to a host of other problems. For example, children who are disciplined with spanking are more likely to become aggressive themselves. Children who are constantly yelled at often become withdrawn and insecure. And shaming a child leads them to feel embarrassed, and unworthy. They argue that such tactics tend to lead to low self-esteem and anxiety.

Therefore, if you want to effectively discipline your toddler, it's best to avoid negative methods. Instead, they encourage that parents try using positive reinforcement and redirection. Positive reinforcement encourages children to make better choices by being praised for good behavior and redirecting helps them focus on more productive things.

So, what is the best way to discipline our children? There is no easy answer, but positive discipline– which focuses on teaching and reinforcement rather than punishment– is often considered the most effective approach. This involves setting clear expectations, providing consistent consequences for misbehavior, and showing your child love and support even when they make mistakes. With patience and understanding, you can help your child learn and grow positively in a healthy way.

If you've got the long-term in mind, then positive discipline is your guy. Research shows that children with loving and kind parents tend to do well in life and will most likely **not** engage in socially risky behaviors.

It goes without saying that positive discipline requires your time and intentional effort. Time. Because there are times you won't feel like you have the time to engage your child in a conversation about why we don't bite others, and so on, but positive discipline requires you to go down this lane. On the other end of the spectrum, you will need to intentionally avoid taking the easy route of yelling, shaming, and spanking. Although this may cause your child's cooperation in the short term, it isn't quite effective in the long term.

All this was foreign concept to us until we understood that we discipline because we love, not because we are angry. And that's when we began our positive discipline journey.

Here's how you can get started with positive discipline

We know all of this might seem daunting at first. And actually, it does take a reasonable effort. That said, the easier way to remember is that positive discipline is more about subconsciously discouraging bad behaviors you don't want to see in your child.

And, guess how you can do this?

You can do this by making your child have a sense of belonging. Let us put this into perspective.

Have you ever worked on a project where although you weren't the team lead, you were involved in generating the ideas the project was built upon?

When it was time to implement these ideas, how connected did you feel to the project?

I bet you felt so connected that you could keep late nights to ensure the project was successful. In this case, what happened was that you began feeling a sense of belonging. You felt like it was your project even though you were not the lead.

In the same way, when you make your child feel a sense of belonging, it is easier to get your child to produce the results you desire. Breathe, take a few seconds to analyze the challenge you are facing at the moment, listen, hug your child, and remind them you are in this together.

At the root level, this is the law of reciprocity at work!

To sum it up, the five ways to start being a parent who engages in positive discipline are:

- Be kind but firm. Even when misbehavior happens, correct your child with love.
- Consciously promote a sense of belonging. Look for ways to make your child feel loved and connected to you and the family.
- Think long-term. The goal isn't just to stop the behavior through punishments. You want your child to develop the ability to choose good behaviors over bad ones. Hence, allow your toddler to make use of their personal powers. Teach your child that they are capable of

making decisions. Make it clear that with these decisions come good or bad consequences.

- At the core, you are teaching your toddler vital life skills. Essential skills such as problem-solving, accountability, and cooperation cannot be overestimated.

Let's dive a bit deeper into the subject of positive discipline as we explore five tested-and-trusted techniques that will give your positive discipline journey a massive boost.

THE 5 POSITIVE DISCIPLINE TECHNIQUES THAT ARE WORTH YOUR TIME

▷ Redirection

This is based on the concept that kids, including toddlers, don't have a long attention span. This means it is easy to distract them from a seemingly "bad" activity to a new one. Plus, when you redirect your child, you talk about what your child **can** do rather than what your child **should not** do. Really, it's just about what you focus on when communicating with your child.

For instance, if your toddler is about to hit you, instead of saying "no hitting," try instead "how about we practice gently using our hands to pat a teddy bear." You can also redirect by moving your child to a different location. If they are trying to get into the cookie jar, try moving your child to a different room or activity. Better yet, try putting the cookie jar in a place that is not visible to your child.

The takeaway is that redirection works best when you toddler-proof your home as much as possible, so there are fewer things' toddlers can get into trouble with in the first place. And when you do need to redirect, use positive language that toddlers can understand. Finally, be consistent with your redirections. If you allow toddlers to hit sometimes without you redirecting them with similar directions, they will get confused about what is acceptable and what is not acceptable behavior.

▷ **Practice positive reinforcement**

Do you recall what we said about positive reinforcement?

We said that positive reinforcement is more about encouraging good behavior than discouraging bad behavior.

And that's what we aim to do with positive reinforcement. The concept of positive reinforcement means rewarding the good acts of your child in an attempt to encourage more of such actions.

For instance, if your child's playtime is over and it's time to return home from the park, consider granting your toddler's request if they ask for extra time politely, rather than throwing a fit in public.

Why?

This shows your child that asking nicely is a better way of getting a positive response than throwing a tantrum.

▷ Don't be overly complicated

If you want quicker responses from your toddler, communicating your demands calmly using one-word or short phrases will be more effective. For instance, directives like "bedtime" will be more effective than saying, "I want you to go to bed right now. What don't you understand about the fact that its bedtime child? What is taking you so long to go to bed..."?

Also, when you use these one-word directives, resist the urge to repeat yourself multiple times consecutively. This will cause your child to expect multiple directives before obeying you. Continue to use one-word directives but take a beat. Give at least a couple of minutes in between directives.

▷ Time-out and time-ins: the ultimate combo

Many parents know what time-outs mean. But research shows that about 85% of parents are doing it wrong.

When we found out how to do it the right way, plus combine it with time-ins, we knew we had cracked the positive discipline code.

Allow us to explain what we mean.

First, let us begin with why time-outs work and what you might be doing wrong. When you give your child a time-out, you remove your child from a stimulating environment and cause them to be alone. The goal of this is not to act as a form of punishment. Instead, the goal is ultimately to get children to voluntarily put themselves in time-outs before they get into any kind of trouble. In fact, this is a skill that will come in handy later in life; when they are older, they will be able to step out of overwhelming situations, take time to gather themselves, and come back to deal with it better afterwards.

However, most parents get it wrong when they try lecturing their children during time-outs or allow them to play with toys.

Nope. That's not how it should be done.

According to research published in Academic Pediatrics , time-outs should consist of "two kinds of nothing." First, there should be nothing going on. Secondly, there should be nothing your toddler should be able to do about that. To be effective, time-outs should be boring.

What is the goal of a time-out for toddlers?

A toddler's attention span is notoriously short, so it's essential to be strategic when using time-outs as a disciplinary tool. Here are some tips for making time-outs effective with toddlers:

- Keep it short. A toddler's attention span is short, so the time-out should be relatively brief - no more than a minute or two.
- Make it consistent. Every time the toddler exhibits undesirable behavior, follow through with a time-out. This will help the toddler understand that the time-out is a consequence of their actions, and it's there to help them take a breather to gather themselves.
- Keep it a positive notion. Before implementing a time-out, explain to the toddler what behavior is expected of them, and it exists to help them gather themselves, it's not a punishment; it's a time to calm themselves down. This will help avoid confusion and frustration.
- Use positive reinforcement. After the toddler has served their time-out, praise them for following the rules. This will reinforce desired behavior and help the toddler understand that they are capable of behaving appropriately.

With these tips in mind, you can successfully use time-outs to help a toddler learn and grow. On the other end of the rope, time-ins involve interacting and not banishing your child when your child does something wrong. So, instead of sending your child to an isolated area, time-ins might mean taking your toddler on a walk outdoors. Then, after your child is calm, both of you can discuss why what happened was not how they should act, after which you ask them if they would like to take this moment to apologize for their behavior.

Alone, time-ins are effective at promoting good behavior. However, when combined with occasional and effective time-outs, you'd create a fantastic discipline combo.

▷ **Practice selective ignoring**

Perhaps, this sounds utterly opposite to what you think a parent should do. However, in the real sense, selective ignoring means ignoring certain behaviors your child displays.

Initially, this might sound absurd. I mean, doesn't this imply that you will be letting your child get away with negative behaviors such as tantrums or stomping?

Actually, yes, sometimes you are.

And, for a good reason.

You see, children will go to any length to get what they want, even if it means throwing a tantrum. When you give in to these ways of asking for things, guess what you are doing? You are providing positive reinforcement for that behavior.

This is the message you are passing across: "I see that you are trying to get what you want right now by throwing a tantrum. So, I will give you what you want, so you, stop, and any other time you throw a tantrum to get my attention to give you what you want."

Of course, not literally. But every time you give in to your child's "negative" way of requesting something, you are sending a message that it's okay to do it.

On the other hand, your child will realize that such methods don't work when you selectively ignore such behavior. Without your audience, the negative behaviors won't seem as appealing to your child. Selective ignoring your toddler means choosing to ignore certain behaviors that are not harmful and do not require immediate attention. However, you must have a positive relationship with your child for this to be effective. What good will it be if you don't give them your attention if they are used to not having your attention? Give your child lots of positive attention when they are behaving well and selectively ignoring bad acts will be an effective consequence.

For instance, if your toddler is whining about a new toy at the supermarket, you can calmly say, "yes, you can have it for your birthday," and continue going about your business. To be honest, this may probably turn into a tantrum the first couple of times you put it into practice, but if you continue to stand your ground and keep giving your child the same answers, eventually they will give in. This will help teach your toddler that tantrums are not a license to getting things.

Selective ignoring can be a tool not only to help reduce toddler tantrums, but also for power struggles in the long run, as it sends the message that the way they behave matters. Again, of course there are times when you should NOT practice selective ignoring with your toddler. If your toddler is engaging in harmful or dangerous behavior, you should always act and address the situation immediately. Additionally, if your toddler is acting out due to hunger, thirst, fatigue, or pain, you should also take steps to address their needs immediately.

In general, practice selective ignoring with your toddler when they are engaged in minor nuisance behaviors that are not harmful and do not require immediate attention. This will help teach them patience and self-control.

Let us tell you a "lovely" little secret.

Do you know how you will know your selective ignoring tactic is working?

Whenever the behavior gets worse, you are on the right path. But still, don't be tricked into giving in at this point just yet. If you do, you will be shooting yourself in the foot.

Why?

When you give in as the tantrum becomes worse, you will be positively reinforcing the wrong act at its peak. This will encourage them to be resilient in their tantrum as they will learn that if they persist just a little longer, you will easily give in. Trust us, they are incredibly clever little creatures!

To balance this, if your child hits, bites, or displays any other acts of aggression, don't practice selective ignoring. Instead, stop these behaviors immediately and consider using other positive discipline tactics such as losing privileges and time-outs.

A MUCH BETTER WAY OF DEALING WITH NEGATIVE BEHAVIOR MORE POSITIVELY.

You are a parent.

And this means you want the best for your child instinctively. So, this means "fixing" the bad behaviors so that your child can have the best possible life.

But is it possible that you are making these mistakes when dealing with the negative behaviors in your toddler?

▷ **Mistake 1#: You search for what you fear**

It's so easy to do this as parents.

I mean, isn't that our job?

Wrong.

More often than not, we fear that our children will go through the same pain or take the same wrong route we did as children. And rightly so. We do this with the best of intentions.

However, although a great tool to curb bad habits, this turns us into behavior-crawlers, constantly looking for signs of certain traits.

And unfortunately, you will often find what you fear-even though it was a positive trait.

If, for instance, you spent most of your childhood being a socially awkward kid, it is normal for you to want your child to be more social. However, if you are teaching your child the importance of time-outs, and suddenly, you see your toddler stepping away from the other kids on the playground, you could easily conclude that your child is following in your childhood footsteps. But that will be wrong.

Most likely you did a great job, and they just want some time to breathe.

So, stop searching for what you fear.

▷ **Mistake 2#: Maybe you've got the wrong lenses on**

Have you ever tried walking on the streets with a blue lens on?

How do you view the world? What color do you see everywhere?

Blue…, right?

Yes. Likewise, maybe that negative behavior is not really negative. Maybe, just maybe, it could be a positive behavior if you flip your lenses.

For instance, if you've got a naughty child who barely follows the directives you give, you could view this as your child being defiant. However, on the flip side, maybe you've got a strong child who won't be afraid to say no to peer pressure.

Do you understand?

All you've got to do right now is to agree always to have a positive outlook on your child's behavior. Like the last point, if you search for what you fear, you will find what you fear. But, if you look at it from the bright side first, most likely you are right.

To draw a line, this doesn't mean you will ignore negative behaviors. Again, that's not why you are doing this. However, seeing the positive aspect doesn't just help you get angry less; it also helps you encourage that "positive" aspect when communicating with your child.

For instance, after throwing a tantrum because you said it was bedtime, during your discussion with your toddler (remember, this is non-negotiable), ask your child what the reason for not wanting to go to bed is. If your toddler gives a tangible reason, that's a good sign; you've got a toddler who's thinking independently (do you see where the positive thinking comes in?). You can then praise your child for this "positive thinking" behavior (positive discipline involves the use of praises, don't forget). Then, you can finally tell your child why it's important to go to bed when you say so.

Although you are encouraging the positives, you are also setting limits around the negatives.

Okay, let's talk about the next mistake.

▷ Mistake #3: You aren't comfortable with different

It's far easier to agree with and love someone who behaves exactly like you.

But, if you want to raise an independent kid, won't this mean that you will have to be comfortable with raising a kid who is different?

"Different" in the sense that your kid thinks or acts differently as you would act. But the difference is not negative.

If there's any behavior in your child that isn't like yours but still isn't likely to cause any future problems, let your child be.

Don't confuse "different" with "negative."

▷ Mistake #4: You view your child as an adult

Unsurprisingly, this is a very common mistake.

As adults, it is customary to think like adults. However, you should keep in mind that your toddler is still a child. And because of this, your toddler will think- and often act- in ways that show that you've still got a child in the house.

For instance, if your toddler wants to have a new toy because it's the character he saw in a movie and you can't get the toy for them, you might be tempted to get angry when your child suddenly begins to throw a fit.

But, if you can put yourself in your child's shoes, what do you see?

You see a little child who wants a new toy and does not yet fully grasp that they can't have everything they want.

And honestly, even if you don't remember, we can all admit we did that as a child.

So, yeah. Take a breath, step into your toddler's shoes, and think as your child does for a moment. Suddenly, you will begin to connect the dots as to why you must deal with a tantrum episode every day. Plus, this helps you come from an emphatic point of view during your conversation with your child.

If you aren't making any of those mistakes, that's great! But if so, welcome to the real parenting club; it's time to go back to the drawing board and map out a new plan with these tips in mind.

You might also want to keep some of the practical examples we will be discussing next.

LET'S BE PRACTICAL: DEALING WITH COMMON DISCIPLINE PROBLEMS

While we may have covered most of the positive discipline techniques you need in this chapter, some issues might require a more streamlined solution. And that's what we are about to dive into now.

▷ Biting

For toddlers, biting is an outlet for an inbuilt frustration or a passionate expression. Hence, it is still a form of communication, even though it isn't the most appropriate one. As they are not in complete control of their emotions, they are just trying to express what they feel inside when they bite.

So, whether they turn their teeth on you, their siblings, or their friends, the goal is to teach them that biting is not a great way of communication and replace their frustration with words.

So, how can you show your toddler that biting is not acceptable?

Whenever your toddler bites you, using words like "Ouch! and "That hurts!" conveys the message of disdain in the act. You could also try to move physically farther from your child.

If your child bites another person, caring for the bitten and not the biter will show your toddler that biting is not a great way of expression. It will be a lot more effective when you request an apology from your child.

As regards to replacing your toddler's frustration with words, whenever you realize your child is frustrated by an event, use this formula: "I know you are frustrated about [event] but [reason for the event]." For instance, if you need your child to stop playing and get into the shower, you could say, "I know you are frustrated that you have to stop playing with your toys, but you need to get into the shower and get ready, so we don't get to the birthday party late my love."

Doing this will help your toddler associate the raging feeling inside with the word "frustration," giving your child a word to use whenever the feeling pops in their head again.

▷ **Hitting & Kicking**

There's no bad child; there are just bad behaviors. You need to approach this **not** from a "my child is aggressive" point of view but from the "I need to show my child better ways of communicating frustration" point of view.

Like biting, when a kid hits or kicks another person, it is an attempt to communicate frustration. Hence, following the two-step approach we used in solving biting won't be a bad try.

First, you need to show your child that hitting, and kicking isn't a good way of communicating. Saying "Ouch" followed by "We don't hit other people" is a great place to start.

Secondly, teach your toddler useful coping mechanisms and techniques that can be used when the feeling to hit comes back again. "Whenever you feel like hitting, put your hands in your pocket or find a pillow so you can let your frustrations out," followed by "Remember we don't hit people, we are kind to one another."

Do you see how we are not approaching this as an angry parent but as a loving parent trying to correct bad behavior? Now, that's positive parenting.

▷ **Lying**

There's always a reason behind a lie. Children don't just lie- Lies are often told in an attempt to escape rejection, punishment, or a disappointed parent. However, lying should not be confused with a wild imagination, which is a normal part of early childhood.

We know it might be tricky at first trying to differentiate these two. However, lies are mostly told to prevent some sort of penalty.

To deal with lies, you must first address the root cause of the lie. Find out the reason why your child is lying. Could it be that your response to imperfection is a bit harsh? Children often lie to avoid a disappointed parent.

Secondly, try to be as honest as possible. "I don't think that's the truth" is a great way to interrupt a lie. Encourage your child to tell the truth and reward them when the truth is spoken. "I love how you spoke the truth at the playground; keep it up."

▷ **Back Talking**

If there's anything we know about children, it is that they are bluntly honest. And we figured that's why they talk back most of the time.

Your child doesn't talk back to oppose your authority. Look back- In the past, whenever your child talked back, it was, most likely, because the idea you presented did not sound inviting.

When this happens, saying "Let's give that a try again" will show your child that back talking isn't an acceptable response. Plus, since back talking is often their opinion expressed as blunt as it could, giving children another chance helps them deliver their opinion in a better way.

▷ **Interrupting**

Again, let's treat the root cause of the problem rather than the problem itself. When toddler's interrupt, it all boils down to one fact- children feel their significance is threatened when your attention is focused somewhere else.

So, dealing with interrupting should be about reminding your child that while they won't always have your attention, your love is a constant in their lives. Plus, this should be done before the phone call begins.

First, find ways to keep your toddler busy before beginning a conversation with someone else. "Look, your friends are playing over there. Do you want to go hang out with them?"

Secondly, talk to your child about why interrupting is not nice or appreciated. Every discussion can wait until after your conversation is over (except if it is an emergency). Having this discussion before your conversation begins is better than barking a "don't interrupt" order during the conversation. It helps them understand that they should respect that you are having a conversation.

▷ **Bossiness**

It's not uncommon for toddlers to be bossy. They are just beginning to learn about the world around them and how to assert themselves. As a parent, it's vital to help your toddler learn how to be a leader instead of being bossy. Some kids are natural-born leaders. So, it won't come as a surprise to see these kids leading the way in playgrounds. However, managing a playground boss teaches children better ways to communicate.

And this begins at home. So here are some actionable tips to help you coach your toddler into being a leader:

- Encourage your toddler to express their ideas and feelings. This will help them feel heard and understood.
- Teach your toddler how to listen to others. This includes giving them attention, making eye contact, and taking turns talking.
- Model respectful behavior yourself. This means speaking kindly, listening carefully, and being considerate of others' feelings.
- Encourage your toddler to cooperate with others. This includes playing games, doing puzzles, and sharing toys.
- Help your toddler learn how to resolve conflicts. This can be done by teaching them

how to use words to express their needs, listening to what others have to say, and finding compromises.

For instance, when your toddler wants to express their ideas, ask them questions such as "What do you think we should do?" or "How do you feel about that?" This will help them to think about their ideas and feelings more deeply.

By following these tips, you can help your toddler learn to be a leader instead of being bossy.

▷ Whining

This is a toddler's way of communicating that they are unhappy or want something. While it can be frustrating for parents, there are some practical ways to deal with it.

First, it's important to try and figure out what the toddler is trying to communicate. They may be hungry, tired, or just need some attention. Once you know the reason for the whining, you can better address it.

If the toddler is hungry, try offering them a snack or drink. If they are tired, see if they will take a nap or have some quiet time. And if they just need some attention, spend some quality time with them playing or hugging them.

Sometimes, no matter what you do, the toddler will still whine. It's important to stay calm and distract them with nature or an object. Dealing with a toddler's whining can be challenging, but by remaining patient and understanding, you can help them (and yourself) through it.

▷ Tattling

This is the act of telling on someone else, usually to get them in trouble. It's commonly seen in toddlers, who are still learning the rules of social interactions. While it may be annoying to parents, it's a normal part of child development.

Tattling can become a problem if it's excessive or done with malicious intent (which is hardly the reason). If your child is constantly tattling on their siblings or friends, it can create tension and conflict. Likewise, if your child is using tattling to get others in trouble, it's important to nip that behavior.

So, what should you do if your toddler starts tattling? First, try to redirect them by saying, "remember, we are not tattle tales." This does wonders in teaching them that tattling is not cool. If that doesn't work, have a calm discussion about why tattling isn't appreciated, especially if they have older siblings. If this is the case at your home, encourage your toddler to be good friends with their sibling. You may say to your toddler, "you want to be your [sibling name] friend, and if you keep on being a tattle tale, they might not appreciate it." The goal is to avoid sibling rivalry from an early age. Finally, praise your child when they refrain from tattling.

With patience and this practical guidance, your toddler will outgrow this phase. Before you know it, you will hear your toddler saying to their little friends, "don't be a tattle tale, don't be a tattle tale…"

▷ **Sibling conflicts**

This is inevitable if you've got more than a kid in the house. Why? When you ask two humans who always want things to go their way, having a conflict is normal. But, although conflicts are normal, the rivalry doesn't have to be.

Teach your children to acknowledge each other's gifts and see each other point of view whenever they are in an argument while still validating the feelings they have. This teaches your children a skill that can be employed in arguments as they grow older. "It's okay to be angry, but that doesn't mean you are right."

Though they are a normal part of growing up, sibling conflicts can be frustrating and even dangerous. As parents, it is important to know how to handle these situations effectively and address them at an early age.

The first step is to stay calm. It can be easy to get caught up in the emotion of the situation, but it is essential to remember that children often mirror the behavior of adults. If you remain calm, it will be easier for your children to do the same.

Next, try to understand what started the conflict. Was there a disagreement about a toy? Did one child feel left out? Once you know the root cause of the conflict, you can start to work on a solution.

If the conflict is about a toy or other object, you may need to intervene and help the children share. If the conflict is due to feelings of jealousy or insecurity, you may need to spend more time with each child individually to help them feel loved and valued.

The chances are that the conflict is mostly due to the reasons mentioned above, but no matter the cause of the sibling conflict, it is important always to encourage their friendship. This means praising children when they get along and providing constructive criticism when conflicts arise. By teaching your children how to handle conflict effectively, you can help them develop into well-rounded adults. As guess what? The chances are that they will not always see eye to eye with others as they grow up.

Again, why intervene only when your children argue? The thing is children love attention. And any behavior you pay attention to will be reinforced. Hence, encouraging your kids when they are having a blissful play together will be effective. "I love how you and your brother are getting along!"

INTERACTIVE ELEMENT- SUMMARY

- Positive discipline means you discipline because you love your child, not because you are angry.
- Practice positive reinforcement when you engage with your toddler. When your toddler displays behaviors, you approve of, offer praise.
- Don't fall into the trap of searching for what you fear. Often, you will find what you are looking for.
- The lenses through which you view your child's behaviors matter. Could you be more positive?

In summary, the sixth step to managing anger is identifying the most common situations your toddler struggles with and practicing positive discipline. The earlier you start, the sooner you will see positive results.

Knowing what you do now, how can you respond differently? How can you approach the behavior you dislike with a positive discipline approach?

That said, is your present home environment optimized for living with a toddler? In the next chapter, you'll learn how to create a positive environment suitable for your toddler at home.

7

A POSITIVE HOME

In the last six chapters, we've covered tips for managing your anger.

As we conclude in this chapter, we believe it is time we move past the "how" of anger management and go deeper into the "why" of anger management.

At the root of it, most of us don't want to be angry parents because we want our children to grow up in a positive home- a home that supports proper childhood development. And, as you will see, the more of such an environment you can create the less angry situations you will encounter. This is because not only will you have a more cooperative child, but you will subconsciously realize that your core desire is being fulfilled, day by day.

It is critical for the healthy development of children to have a haven where they can feel physically, socially, and emotionally secure. Plus, children who develop the proper bond with their parents often exhibit fewer risky behaviors later in life.

Every parent desires that their little one grows up in such a home. But only a few are making conscious efforts to bring it to reality. However, since you've shown your dedication to creating such a home for your child, let's dive into techniques that will help you provide the right environment for your little buddy.

WHAT ARE THE FACTORS THAT AFFECT A CHILD'S DEVELOPMENT?

▷ **Family bonding and connection**

In the age of technology, it is easy to leave our children to spend their hours on YouTube or TV. However, you must ensure this doesn't happen to your child. Spending time and having physical contact with your child is essential for creating a positive home for your children.

With the loads of work, we've got to do, we know how difficult this might sound. You might be tempted to use technology as an escape route from your toddler but limit that to the bare minimum. Create intentional family time in your schedule, as this connection is essential for a toddler's development.

Designate specific days or periods of the week as family time. This will let your toddler know that this is a special quality time that they can look forward to. It's lovely to have movie night together. But don't just watch television or movies together, engage in other activities that everyone can enjoy. This could be playing games, cooking, or even going for walks together.

The goal is to make sure to focus on your toddler and give them your undivided attention. Encourage communication and bonding by asking questions, telling stories, and sharing experiences.

Likewise, family bonding doesn't only refer to building a relationship with your little one, even though it involves that. Family bonding also means preventing big arguments between family members. Children who grow up in homes with constant arguments often have trouble making friends later. So, it's essential to end family time on a positive note, such as by expressing gratitude for one another or sharing something you enjoyed about the experience.

In the beginning that we started doing this, it was a bit awkward for us. As we didn't grow up in a home where a time for expressing gratitude took place, it was new to us. However, it didn't take long before we heard our children expressing gratitude to one another. Now, we hear them thank each other for several things, like getting water for one another, or even when we cook for them, we hear them say "thank you for cooking for me." And this happens without us having to "pressure" them to do so. So, expressing gratitude for one another has been powerful tool for creating a positive home for us.

▷ Physical environment

The importance of your child's physical environment cannot be overemphasized. The physical environment plays a critical role in a child's development. The way a toddler interacts with their surroundings can profoundly impact their cognitive, social, and emotional development.

For example, research has shown that children who have opportunities to explore and engage with their environment are more likely to develop higher self-control and executive function skills. Furthermore, children who have access to stimulating and supportive environments are more likely to develop strong social and emotional skills.

The physical environment is thus a crucial part of a toddler's development and can impact their future in several ways. Therefore, it is crucial for parents to create an environment conducive to their child's development and provide them with opportunities to explore and engage with their surroundings.

There are many ways you can do this. Build their space environment according to your home space. Ensure that there are no sharp objects or dangerous chemicals within reach, and create a specific space with children's wall art, free of clutter with plenty of soft, comfortable places to play and explore.

▷ **Financial situation**

Let's not underestimate the importance of money when raising kids. A toddler's home environment should not be only emotionally but also financially stable. While it may not be the most important thing, living under your means with a plan on how to administrate your money can help reduce stress for parents, which creates a more positive home environment for kids.

In today's society, the cost of living is constantly rising. This puts a lot of pressure on families, especially those with young children. Ensuring your toddler has a safe and secure place to call home is important for their development and future success. Creating a financially stable environment is one way to help make this happen. Parents need to remember that they are not alone in this battle. Many organizations and resources are available to help families financially plan or get through tough financial times. Do a search according to your needs.

Some parents may feel ashamed or embarrassed to ask for help, but it is important to remember that there is no shame in admitting that you need assistance. The most important thing is that your toddler has a safe and secure home environment. No matter your financial situation, the most important thing is to create a safe and loving home environment for your toddler.

▷ Health and Nutrition

As a parent, you have the ability to shape your toddler's eating habits for years to come. Ensuring that your toddler gets the nutrients, they need to grow strong and healthy is crucial. As much as you care for the external environment of your child, it's even more vital that you care for the internal environment. By this, we mean the body of your toddler. There's so much junk food out there, but don't be tempted to load your child's body with all of that.

When it comes to keeping our toddlers healthy and well-nourished, we need to ensure they get all the essential nutrients their little bodies need. Here are some of the key nutrients that are important for toddler health and some tips on how to make sure your toddler is getting enough of them:

Vitamin A: Vitamin A is essential for vision, immune function, and cell growth. Good sources of vitamin A include sweet potatoes, carrots, eggs, and dairy products.

Iodine: Iodine is essential for thyroid function and brain development. Seafood, dairy products, and eggs are all excellent sources of iodine.

Iron: Iron is essential for cognitive development, energy levels, and healthy blood cells. Good sources of iron include red meat, dark leafy greens, beans, and nuts.

Calcium: Calcium is essential for strong bones and teeth. Good sources of calcium include dairy products, leafy greens, and almonds.

Make sure your toddler is getting all the essential nutrients they need by including various nutrient-rich foods in their diet. By doing so, you'll be setting them up for a lifetime of good health!

▷ **Learning**

School or daycare shouldn't be the only place your child gets to learn. It would be best to teach your child that the world presents different learning avenues every day. Your child can learn from everything and everywhere if you train your child to ask questions.

Yes, teaching your child to ask questions is a great way to spur your child's learning process. This also means that when your child asks you questions with self-evident answers (for example, "why is water wet?"), answer the little champ.

▷ **Mental environment**

Giving your children a safe physical environment is not everything. You must also ensure your kid's mental space is secure and suitable for a toddler. If screen time is just unavoidable, make sure that your children's TV shows and YouTube channels are toddlers appropriate. Screen them and ensure they are safe for your child.

We live in a time when it is essential to create a mentally stimulating environment at home for a toddler. This can be done in several ways, but some key things to keep in mind are encouraging communication and interaction, offering a variety of activities, and creating opportunities for pretend play.

Encouraging communication means providing opportunities for your toddler to talk, listen, and practice their language skills. This can be done through simple conversations, singing songs, and reading books together.

A variety of activities will help your toddler explore different ways of thinking and problem-solving. Try to offer a mix of active and passive activities and some that encourage creative expression. One that we love is memory games. Games like Simon Says or Memory are great for helping toddlers exercise their thinking and problem-solving memory muscles.

Pretend play is an excellent way for toddlers to practice new skills and make sense of the world around them. It can also be a lot of fun! Encourage your toddler to use their imagination by providing simple props and toys that can be used in various ways.

By creating a mentally stimulating environment at home, you will help your toddler develop critical cognitive skills and lay the foundation for a lifetime of learning.

BUILDING A POSITIVE MENTAL SPACE FOR YOUR CHILD

▷ **Shower them with positive praise**

How do you feel when you hear words of affirmation from a friend? Delightful, right? Now imagine if your child gets this from you all day long! This is a two-edged sword because, first, it just really makes your child happy, and second, it provides positive reinforcement for the behaviors you love. Naturally your child enjoys seeing you happy, the more they are praised for positive behaviors, the more they are motivated to replicate them. This means they will start doing less of what triggers your anger, resulting in fewer yells.

▷ Be affectionate

Let your child know you love them with warm hugs and kisses. Research shows that toddlers with affectionate parents have a larger hippocampus- the part of the brain responsible for learning and stress management. So, guess what, be affectionate. Go ahead, smooch and snuggle that little munchkin because there's no such a thing as being too loving with your children.

▷ Turn your home into a gallery

Hang inspirational children's wall art on the wall as well as your kid's artwork where they can see it. Children relate to what they see differently than adults do. What children see at a young age becomes engraved in their souls. Displaying animal artwork with a positive message or your child's diagram of a fish on your refrigerator can significantly boost your child's confidence levels. Hang it closer to where they spend most of their time so that they can have a peek while they play. It will inspire immense creativity in your toddler.

Try it and watch as they stare at it. It will do wonders to their imagination. Not to mention that based on what you see today in the art world, you can also go and turn those little pen scribbles into a million-dollar work of art in the future! (wink)

▷ **Be huge on self-love.**

I'm sure you want to raise a kid who understands the importance of self-love. If we had our way, we all have something we wish we could change about ourselves. But since we don't, merely thinking about our insufficiency will do us more harm than good. And this applies to your child too.

The best way to encourage self-love in your home is to show it. Those little side comments such as "I wish I looked like so and so" will ultimately imprint a destructive mindset on your child. Instead, focus on what you can improve daily from a place of self-love.

▷ **Give them your time**

You've heard this repeatedly in this book. The importance of spending time with your toddler cannot be overemphasized. But remember that quality triumphs over quantity. If you will do it at all, be present at the moment.

IT'S ABOUT CREATING A STRUCTURE

Just so you know, building a positive home won't happen because of a single discussion or a single effort. You need to be intentional about creating a structure at home. Creating a positive home environment for your toddler means having a safe, predictable, and consistent space. It means establishing rules and limits and providing plenty of love and support.

Hence, planning, consistency, predictability, and follow-through are key. Without planning you are planning to fail. Rules and routines create consistency, while predictability comes from knowing what will happen next. Following through with consequences, enforce the rules and help keep toddler tantrums to a minimum.

Creating a positive home environment for your toddler doesn't have to be complicated. Just focus on creating structure, and you'll be well on your way to raising a happy, healthy child.

Although these four tenets are intertwined, your rules won't be effective without them. There are five types of rules toddlers need in a home when talking about rules. Are you lacking any of these?

▷ **Safety rules**

These include both physical and emotional safety. An example of a physical safety rule could be "don't eat anything given by a stranger," while an example of an emotional safety rule could be "It's Okay to be frustrated. But, you need to talk to me about it."

▷ **Healthy habit rules**

What we did at our home was create the 10 family health commandments, but remember every family is different; therefore, it's important to adapt them accordingly. The commandments in our house go like this:

1. Thou shalt eat breakfast every day.
2. Thou shalt brush thy teeth after breakfast and before going to bed.
3. Thou shalt take a nap every afternoon.
4. Thou shalt play outside every day.
5. Thou shalt eat thy veggies at dinner.
6. Thou shalt go to bed by 8 pm.
7. Thou shalt drink lots of water throughout the day.
8. Thou shalt eat healthy snacks in between meals.
9. Thou shalt have family dinners together.
10. Thou shalt always take the stairs.

Breakfast is the most important meal, and toddlers should start their day with a nutritious meal to fuel their growing bodies. After every breakfast and before bed, brushing their teeth will help keep those pearly whites healthy and avoid cavities.

A daily afternoon nap will help the toddler recharge and be ready for more fun. Outdoor play is vital for fresh air and exercise. Eating veggies at dinner is a crucial part of a healthy diet, and a toddler should try to eat them every day.

Going to bed by 8 pm will help your toddler get the recommended minimum of 10 hours of sleep per night. Drinking lots of water throughout the day is essential for staying hydrated and keeping their bodies functioning properly.

Healthy snacks like fruits and vegetables are a great way to tide your hungry bear until their next meal.

Family dinners are a great time to bond and catch up while enjoying a healthy meal.

Taking the stairs instead of the elevator is a great way to promote an active lifestyle from a young age. This will also apply to parking the car far away when you go grocery shopping. Your toddler will most likely ask, "why did we stop so far away?" and you will have the opportunity to respond, "because walking is very good for our health!".

The goal is to get your child indoctrinated into habits that promote a lifestyle of healthy habits from an early age. Following these simple rules will help your toddler develop healthy habits that will last a lifetime.

▷ Social skill rules

When it comes to social skills, toddlerhood is a crucial time. During these years, children learn how to interact with others, share and take turns, and resolve conflicts. Let's discuss some simple rules to help your toddler develop strong social skills.

- Encourage turn-taking: When your toddler is playing with a toy, let them play with it for a little while before asking for another child to have a turn. This will help them learn to share and take turns with others.
- Model kindness and empathy: Model the behaviors you want your toddler to display. If they see you being kind and empathetic, they are more likely to mimic those behaviors.
- Use role playing. If you see you child is having difficulty sharing for example, you may role play with your partner. "Here's my book, I will share it with you so you can enjoy it for a while as well." This is one of the strongest ways to

help your toddler- role playing. It can apply to almost anything in toddlerhood.

- Encourage cooperation: Try to encourage cooperative play rather than competitive play. For example, instead of racing your toddler to the finish line, you may make it a relay race instead.
- Respect your toddler's feelings: It's important to respect your toddler's feelings and emotions. If they are upset, try to understand why and offer comfort. This will help them learn to cope with and express their feelings.

Following these simple rules will help your toddler develop strong social skills that will serve them well throughout their life.

▷ **Morality rules**

These are rules that help your child develop morals in life. A list of examples could be as simple as:

- We are kind, we don't hit others.
- We are caring. We share with our friends.
- We are sincere. We say sorry when we make a mistake.
- We are honest. We tell the truth always.

- We are compassionate. We help others when they need it.
- We are loving. We are nice to animals.
- We are respectful. We respect our elders.
- We are leaders. We do our absolute best, and if we need help, we ask nicely.
- We are role models. We carry ourselves in a way that has a positive impact on others.

These are just a few basic toddler morality rules that should be followed to help them develop into well-rounded, moral individuals. It's crucial to instill these values at a young age so that they can carry them with them throughout their lives. Try to discuss with your toddler why following these rules are important and how it will make them and those around them happy. Lead by example and praise your toddler when they display acts of kindness, honesty, or helpfulness. With your guidance, they will develop into powerful individuals in no time!

▷ **Real-world Preparedness**

These are rules that prepare your toddler for the real world. The truth is, it is not all rosy out there and teaching your child essential life skills to survive is vital. What are those rules? Well, I'm glad you asked.

Let's discuss 10 examples that you can still in your toddler early on:

1. Don't put anything in your mouth that doesn't belong there. This includes fallen food on the floor, rocks, sticks, leaves, and bugs.
2. If it's not yours, don't not take it. This goes for toys, electronics, books, and art supplies. If you see something you want, ask nicely first.
3. Be careful with people's things. Treat them with respect and care, just as you would want your own things to be treated.
4. Keep your hands and feet to yourself. That means no hitting, kicking, pushing, or biting.
5. Be kind with your words. No name-calling, teasing, or mean comments.
6. Be a good listener. When someone is talking to you, give them your full attention and try to understand what they're saying.
7. Follow the rules. Whether it's at home, school, or somewhere else, it's important to obey the rules and do what's expected of you.
8. Use your manners. Please, thank you, and excuse me are a few magic words that will make people want to be around you.

9. Be considerate of others. Think about how your actions will affect others before you do something.

10. Be tolerant of differences. We're all different, which makes the world an exciting place. Accepting and celebrating our differences is what makes us human.

And how about masterful rules every home needs? Fair enough, let's go in to five rules every home need and how you can develop them.

MASTERING THE ART OF DEVELOPING FAMILY RULES

There are four steps to creating a world-class family rule. They are:

- Identifying the rules
- Explaining the rules
- Following through on the rules
- Using the consequences of the rules not followed.

Let's deal with this one after the other.

▷ Identify the family rules

This is when you introduce the new rule to your toddler. There are a few keyways to identify the family rules for your toddler.

Firstly, it is important to be clear and consistent with your toddler about what the expectations are in your household. This means that every family member should be on the same page about the rules and that everyone should enforce them in the same way. As much as possible, avoid using vague concepts such as "Be good." Instead, be as specific as possible. If you want your child to be at sleep at a set time, say, "Starting today, bedtime routine will start by 6:30 P.M, and this will repeat every night, little one."

Start with one or two rules and add more gradually. Don't overburden your child with too many directions all at once.

Secondly, it is helpful to use positive reinforcement when your toddler follows the rules. This could include verbal praise, hugs, or gifts. Don't panic; the gifts can be something as simple as a removable sticker.

Thirdly, it is important to avoid physical punishment when enforcing the rules. This can include spanking, slapping, or hitting.

Finally, it is crucial to be patient and understanding with your toddler when they are learning the rules. It takes time for toddlers to understand and follow the rules, so it is essential to be patient and keep working with them. Remember, creating a structure is a gradual process.

▷ **Explain the rules**

Here's where you and your child have discussions about the rules. Explaining rules to your toddler can be tricky. You need to ensure your child understands the rule. Tips to follow include:

- Explain why you are setting the rule.
- Keep it simple. Use short, concise sentences when explaining the rule.
- Toddlers don't easily slide into new routines & rules. So, you might need to set up reminders (a visual reminder is often better).
- Use age-appropriate language. Avoid using words that your toddler may not understand.
- Make it relatable. Use examples or analogies to help your toddler understand the rule.
- Ask your child to explain the rule back to you.
- Be patient. It may take a few times for your toddler to understand the rule. Keep explaining it in different ways until they grasp the concept.

Let's look at an example of how you might explain a simple rule to your toddler:

"No hitting."

"We don't hit because it hurts other people. "

"We are kind to others; even if we disagree, we do not hurt others."

"Sometimes, people might accidentally bump into each other. That's okay. But if we hit someone on purpose, it's not nice."

"Let's try to use our words instead of hitting."

▷ Follow the rules

Here's where discipline comes in. Try to follow through with the rule even when you don't "feel" like doing so. Remember, consistency is key when it comes to building new habits. Therefore, parents need to be consistent in enforcing the rules. If parents are inconsistent with rules, toddlers will learn that they can get away with breaking them. Toddlers will also learn that rules are not important if they are constantly being broken.

Don't forget that toddlers are still learning about the world and how to behave in it. They need clear boundaries and consistent rules to know what is expected of them.

▷ **Use consequences**

This could mean negative or positive consequences. Whichever one it is, ensure you follow through with it. But before we move on, it's important to recall that there are a few things to keep in mind when it comes to toddler rule-breaking. First, toddlers are still learning the rules and may not understand why certain behaviors are unacceptable. Second, toddlers have very short attention spans and may not be able to remember the consequences of their actions for very long. Finally, toddlers' brains are still developing, and they may not be able to control their emotions or impulses very well.

With all of that in mind, let's discuss a few ideas for appropriate consequences for toddler rule-breaking:

- Time-out: This can be an effective consequence for minor infractions like throwing tantrums.
- Loss of privileges: This should be in a timely manner and relatable to the rule broken. If you child continues to throw toys, remove the toy and let them know that they can play with it again when they are ready to do so. This will help them know that there are real consequences for their actions.

- Redirection: For young toddlers who are still learning the rules, sometimes all it takes is a redirection to another activity to get them back on track. If they're hitting, try giving them a soft pillow to hit instead. If they're biting, offer them a teething ring to chew on.

Remember, consequences should be age-appropriate and toddler-specific. With a little creativity, you can find consequences to help your toddler learn the rules and start making better choices.

It's no secret that toddlers can be a handful. They're always living life at a thousand miles per hour, and this can cause stress on parents. However, a schedule creates a wonderful world for a toddler, and as you will guess, it's also lovely for parents. So how do you create a toddler schedule that will work for both you and your little one?

HOW TO MAKE THE PERFECT TODDLER SCHEDULE

Routine cannot be separated from a positive home environment. A toddler thrives on routine and predictability. Having a set schedule helps a toddler feel safe and secure, which leads to fewer tantrums and a general feeling of calmness. Of course, there will always be deviations from the schedule (nap times don't always go as planned, for example), but having a general plan for each day gives a toddler a sense of stability. Again, it's scientifically proven that creating a schedule for your child will help you manage your anger. Here's how- with growing motor skills, toddlers crave independence. This means they won't always do what their parents ask them to do. However, it becomes easier to fall into transitions with a schedule- as though they are the normal thing to do.

So, converting the behavior you want to see in your toddler from an order into a daily routine will go a long way in reducing how much you get angry.

That said, let's dive into the tips for creating the proper schedule:

- Focus on your kid's morning and evening routines first. The key is to begin slowly and gradually progress.
- Does your child love reading time at a particular time? Or napping? Observe their natural tendencies and shape the schedule around them. This will help the routine look natural when in motion.
- A steady sleep and wake-up time is ideal for keeping a routine. Even though you might feel

tempted to let your toddler sleep in, don't. Keep it to their circadian rhythm.

- Naptime is essential. As a general rule of thumb, toddlers should be getting between 12-14 hours of sleep every day, including 1-3 hours of naptime. However, be careful not to schedule naptime close to bedtime.
- You don't need to fill up the entire awake period. It might come naturally to you because you are an adult, and adults love being productive. But, for a toddler just getting familiar with the world, productivity isn't a word that exists. So, factor in quiet time- a period where your toddler can do anything they choose.
- Keep a consistent mealtime routine. Ensure you fill your child's meals with healthy foods.
- Go through the plan with your child. The idea of a routine may be new to your toddler. Begin with why you feel a routine is necessary and explain the routine you are proposing. If your child has any questions, be sure to answer them.
- Don't be so bothered about bumps in the road. Cause' they will come. Definitely. There will be days when unexpected circumstances will come in the way of your schedule. During these days, be flexible. Don't force anything and just move

with the flow of the day. But, you should return to the schedule as soon as possible.

Let's take a look at a routine we once developed for our children.

- **6:30-7:00 am:** Wake up time and get dressed.
- **7-7:30 am** Breakfast. We also turn this into a family bonding time, we talk about any dreams we had and discuss how we would like the day to go.
- **7:30-7:55 am** Playtime. Particularly unstructured play. This kind of play, according to research, is perfect for toddlers. An example of this is playing with simple building blocks.
- **8:00-8:25 am** Drive time. Here's when we commute to school. We take this time to listen to music, audible stories, and observe what we see.
- **8:30 am - 3 pm** School time. We take turns on who will take the kids to school weekly in our house. This helps not overload one person, but of course, every household is unique.
- **3-3:25 pm** The afternoon snack. We always provide healthy snacks for our children, but occasionally, we stop for chocolate or ice cream. (Wink, wink!)

- **3:30-4:25 pm** Playtime. Depending on the weather, this can be at a park, at home, or at a children's age-appropriate play facility.
- **4:30-7 pm** Dinner preparation, dinner time, and family time.
- **7-8 pm**: Nighttime routine such as bath, brushing teeth, bedtime stories, and cuddling.
- **8pm:** Bedtime. Lights out. Good night!

While doing all of this, it's important to keep the home as organized as possible. The key word is "organized," not sparkling clean. This is especially important if you have a toddler. Having a toddler may sometimes seem like a little tornado went through your house; there are toys everywhere, clothes thrown about, and food crumbs on the floor. It's hard enough to keep up with them, let alone worry about cleaning up after them constantly. And honestly, even if you ask them to help you put everything away, guess what? They are still children; most likely it will not go perfectly in its place.

However, an organized home can provide a much-needed sense of calm amid a hectic day for parents. And for children, an organized home can provide a safe and nurturing environment to play and learn. Physical clutter often results in mental clutter. Therefore, an organized place means a clearer mind. So, it's essential to at least keep it organized.

At our home, we used to put so much stress on ourselves because we wanted to do it all; follow the schedule to the minute, be the perfect parents, and have the home clean enough to eat from the counter. Instead of enjoying all the beauty of parenthood, we were over-stressing about the mission impossible. We finally came to our senses and set our priorities in order. Yes, the house should be well cleaned at least once a week, but unless you have a personal helper at home, keeping the house sparkling clean daily is just not realistic.

So, if you are a clean freak and feel overwhelmed by the state of your home, take a deep breath, and focus on what is more important to you, having your home shining or enjoying the most important time in your child's life. Your decision will make a world of difference for your sanity and your family.

INTERACTIVE ELEMENT- SUMMARY

- Creating a positive environment in your home helps diffuse tension and reduce your tendency to get angry.
- Implement the factors that contribute to the positivity of your home environment gradually.

- Creating a toddler schedule helps put your day in order, helps your child transition easier, and sets you free from the constant cycle of yelling.
- Developing a structure that you consistently follow is critical for the healthy development of children where they can feel physically, socially, and emotionally secure. It will go a long way in reducing how much you get angry daily, resulting in a much more pleasant parenthood.

Now, the question is- does your home tick all the boxes listed in this chapter. If it doesn't, it is time to return to the drawing board and come up with a plan and make adjustments. Creating a positive home for your child (and you) is the seventh and most sustainable step for managing anger!

CONCLUSION

We've covered quite a lot in this book. We wanted to make it as real and practical as possible for you. Being parents ourselves we know that parenting is not a walk in the park, and without these tips and tricks, chances are you may have found parenting to be hard. But don't be so hard on yourself. Most parents, including us were in the same boat. Focus on the step-by-step progress of this journey that is called parenthood, not the perfection of it. You are now equipped with all you need to become a rock star parent.

In a jiffy, let's go over the seven steps to managing anger:

Step 1- It starts with you. Take some time to reflect and understand yourself. Learning how to process your emotion is the key to anger management. You might have learned anger as a kid, or you could be getting angry because of your stress levels. Take a deep breath, dive into yourself, and discover why you might be getting angry. Only by addressing your emotions can we hope to resolve future situations in a better way.

Step 2- Understand your child's perspective. This will help you approach challenging moments empathetically when they don't seem to listen to you.

Step 3- Evaluate your parenting style. Is your parenting style supportive of anger management or not? If so, great. If not, make the necessary tweaks.

Step 4- Work towards putting the "magical" 5:1 principle into your life. Don't just focus on reducing the negative interactions. Shift your focus to ramping up the positive interactions you have with your child.

Step 5- Become your child's life coach. When you help your toddler manage the new emerging emotions, you successfully help them ace their developing stages. As they do so, they become more emotionally intelligent and the more emotionally intelligent they are, the faster they mature. The result? It reduces the number of situations that could provoke your anger.

Step 6- Take the positive discipline path. Science backs you up. Identify the most common situations your toddler struggles with and practice disciplining with love. When you do, you'll achieve a much better result.

Step 7- Labor to build a positive home. The environment your toddler grows up in matters not just for your child but also for you. A positive home helps you further the critical goal behind your anger management ordeal. And when this happens, you'll feel more equipped to deal with the everyday situations that would have triggered you.

These seven steps transformed the way we dealt with our children. Before we expected, we were stressing a lot less and enjoying parenthood so much more.

We've shared these tips with lots of our friends, and guess what? They had similar results.

Basically, it works.

Now, it's your turn to go out there (actually, into your home) and get your hands dirty. You can now keep your cool while raising an amazing human.

Really, we hope you can get started on what you've learned from this book. Start applying these tips a step at a time as soon as you can and watch how the results you get will leave you awed.

When you get the results, you hope to get, consider recommending this book to your friends and family so that you all can ace parenting together. Parenting is meant to be a community of compassion and support. Together we are stronger.

Lastly, if you enjoyed this book, kindly leave a review!

To leave quick review just scan the QR code below!

A FREE GIFT FOR MY READERS!

Included with your purchase of this book is your free copy of
7 Morning Rituals That Help Parents Thrive Daily

Scan the QR code below to receive your free copy:

BIBLIOGRAPHY

5 Positive Discipline Strategies to Change Your Child's Behavior. (2021, June 20). Verywell Family. https://www.verywellfamily.com/examples-of-positive-discipline-1095049

A. (2020, September 30). *The Right Way to Get Over the Negative Interactions with Your Kids.* Gurukul. http://gurukultheschool.com/blog/the-right-way-to-get-over-the-negative-interactions-with-your-kids/

Anger and anger management for parents. (2020, June 22). Raising Children Network. https://raisingchildren.net.au/guides/first-1000-days/looking-after-yourself/anger-management-for-parents

Arora, M. (2020, March 13). *5 Important Factors That Influence Early Childhood Development.* FirstCry Parenting. https://parenting.firstcry.com/articles/5-environmental-factors-influencing-early-childhood-development/

Auger, S. (2021, May 15). *Positive Parenting: Understanding the Magic 5:1 Ratio.* Safe Splash Swim School. https://www.safesplash.com/blog/positive-parenting-understanding-the-magic-51-ratio

CDC. (2019a, November 5). *Family Rules | Creating Structure | Essentials | Parenting Information | CDC.* Centers for Disease Control and Prevention. https://www.cdc.gov/parents/essentials/structure/rules.html

CDC. (2019b, November 5). *Quick Tips | Creating Structure | Essentials | Parenting Information | CDC.* Centers for Disease Control and Prevention. https://www.cdc.gov/parents/essentials/structure/quicktips.html

Christiano, D. (2019, September 27). *Which Parenting Type Is Right for You?* Healthline. https://www.healthline.com/health/parenting/types-of-parenting#takeaway

Common discipline problems and solutions. (2022). Baby Gooroo. https://babygooroo.com/articles/common-discipline-problems-solutions

Controlling your anger as a parent. (2020, August). Pregnancy Birth and Baby. https://www.pregnancybirthbaby.org.au/controlling-your-anger-as-a-parent

Holmes, K. A. A. C. P. E. (2022, April 7). *Why Every Parent Should Know the Magic 5:1 Ratio – And How to Do It*. Happy You, Happy Family. https://happyyouhappyfamily.com/how-to-connect-with-your-child/#h-how-to-connect-with-your-child-the-magic-of-the-5-1-ratio

How to Teach Kids Anger Management Skills. (2021, October 17). Verywell Family. https://www.verywellfamily.com/ways-to-teach-your-child-anger-management-skills-1095010

Klepek, K. (2018, May 16). *How to Make a Schedule for Your Toddler*. Nurture Life. https://www.nurturelife.com/blog/how-to-make-toddler-schedule/

LaScala, M., & LaScala, M. (2021, November 2). *Positive Discipline May Be the Key to Getting Your Kids to Behave, Experts Say*. Good Housekeeping. https://www.goodhousekeeping.com/life/parenting/a26754534/positive-discipline/

Li, P. (2022, May 16). *Emotion Coaching: Help Kids Develop Self-Regulation*. Parenting For Brain. https://www.parentingforbrain.com/emotion-coaching-parents/

Love, K. (2019, April 29). *5 Ways To Build A Positive Home & How It Will Benefit Your Children Long-Term » Read Now!* Daily Mom. https://dailymom.com/nurture/5-ways-to-build-a-positive-home-how-it-will-benefit-your-children-long-term/

Mcleod, S. (2018, May 3). *Erik Erikson's Stages of Psychosocial Development*. Simply Scholar Ltd. https://www.simplypsychology.org/Erik-Erikson.html

Meinke, H. (2019, December 30). *Understanding the Stages of Emotional Development in Children*. Rasmussen University. https://www.rasmussen.edu/degrees/education/blog/stages-of-emotional-development/

Morin, A. (2020, September 22). *Establish Rules That Will Help Your Child Become a Responsible Adult*. Verywell Family. https://www.verywellfamily.com/types-of-rules-kids-need-1094871

N. (2022, May 25). *Toddler crying for no reason? Here's how to handle it.* NewFolks. https://www.newfolks.com/stages/toddler-crying-for-no-reason/

Parker, K. (2020, February 12). *The Power of the Magic 5 to 1 Ratio: A Positive Parenting Approach.* Child & Teen Counseling. https://child teencounseling.org/the-power-of-the-magic-5-to-1-ratio-a-posi tive-parenting-approach/

Petrou, A. (2022). *Types of Parenting Styles: Finding Yours and Why It Matters.* Generation Mindful. https://genmindful.com/blogs/mind ful-moments/types-of-parenting-style

Pincus, D. L., & Pincus, D. L. (2021, May 24). *Positive Parenting: 5 Rules to Help You Deal with Negative Child Behavior More Positively.* Empow- ering Parents. https://www.empoweringparents.com/article/posi tive-parenting-5-rules-to-help-you-deal-with-negative-child- behavior-more-positively/

Positive Parenting Connection. (2017, August 10). *Positive Discipline.* https://www.positiveparentingconnection.net/positive-discipline/

Relationships with toddlers: ideas and tips. (2019, December 12). Raising Children Network. https://raisingchildren.net.au/toddlers/connect ing-communicating/connecting/connecting-with-your-toddler

Richardson, J. M. (2021a, July 14). *Why Am I Such an Angry Parent? And, What Can I Do About It?* A Fine Parent. https://afineparent.com/posi tive-parenting-faq/angry-parents.html

Richardson, J. M. (2021b, July 14). *Why Am I Such an Angry Parent? And, What Can I Do About It?* A Fine Parent. https://afineparent.com/posi tive-parenting-faq/angry-parents.html

Silver, N. (2019, August 28). *Help! Why Is My Toddler Angry and What Can I Do to Help Them?* Healthline. https://www.healthline.com/ health/childrens-health/angry-toddler

The Welsh Government Resources Page. (2022). *Understanding and Soothing a Crying Toddler.* GOV.WALES. https://gov.wales/parent ing-give-it-time/guidance-and-advice/tricky-moments-and-behav iours/coping-with-a-crying-toddler

Thomas, S. (2022, January 4). *5 Reasons Why The Home Environment Is So*

Important. This Playful Home. https://thisplayfulhome.com/why-the-home-environment-is-s-important/

Vancouver Island University. (2022). *Managing Anger – Yours and Others | Managing Workplace Conflict | Vancouver Island University | Canada.* https://adm.viu.ca/workplace-conflict/managing-anger-yours-and-others

Vassar, G. (2020, December 10). *How Does A Parent's Anger Impact His or Her Child?* Lakeside. https://lakesidelink.com/blog/lakeside/how-does-a-parents-anger-impact-his-or-her-child/

Why we get so angry at our kids and what we can do about it. (2022). Https://Www.Ahaparenting.Com/Read/Handling-Anger. https://www.ahaparenting.com/read/handling-anger

ZERO TO THREE. (2015, October 29). *I Said I Want the Red Bowl! Responding to Toddlers' Irrational Behavior.* https://www.zerotothree.org/resources/325-i-said-i-want-the-red-bowl-responding-to-toddlers-irrational-behavior

ZERO TO THREE. (2022). *Toddlers and Challenging Behavior: Why They Do It and How to Respond.* https://www.zerotothree.org/resources/326-toddlers-and-challenging-behavior-why-they-do-it-and-how-to-respond

www.ingramcontent.com/pod-product-compliance
Lightning Source LLC
Chambersburg PA
CBHW070700130626
46553CB00005B/1779